Peterborough Ontario
Book 1 in Colour Photos,
Saving Our History
One Photo at a Time

Photography
by Barbara Raué
2015

Series Name:
Cruising Ontario

Book 99: Peterborough Book 1

Cover photo: 359 Downie Street

Series Name: Cruising Ontario
Saving Our History One Photo at a Time
in colour photos

Other Books by Barbara Raue

Coins of Gold

Arrows, Indians and Love

The Life and Times of Barbara
Volume 1: Inventions That Have Enhanced My Life
Volume 2: Entertainment That I Have Enjoyed
Volume 3: East Coast Trips
Volume 4: Olympics Have Always Intrigued Me
Volume 5: Wonders of the World
Volume 6: Caribbean Cruises We Have Enjoyed
Volume 7: Animals
Volume 8: Storms and Other Major Disasters in My Lifetime
Volume 9: Wars, Terrorist Attacks and Major Disasters

The Cromwell Family Book

Laura Secord Discovered

Daddy Where Are You?

Visit Barbara's website to view all of her books
http://barbararaue.ca

Peterborough

Peterborough is a city on the Otonabee River in central Ontario, 125 kilometres (78 miles) northeast of Toronto. Peterborough's nickname of "The Electric City" underscores the historical and present day importance of technology and manufacturing as an economic base of the city which has operations from large multi-national companies such as Seimans, Rolls Royce, and General Electric. Peterborough is known as the gateway to the Kawarthas, "cottage country", a large recreational region of the province. In 1818, Adam Scott settled on the west shore of the Otonabee River and the following year he began construction of a sawmill and gristmill, establishing the area as Scott's Plains. The mill was located at the foot of present-day King Street and was powered by water from Jackson Creek.

The year 1825 marked the arrival of 1,878 Irish immigrants from the city of Cork, a British Parliament experimental emigration plan to transport poor Irish families to Upper Canada. The scheme was managed by Peter Robinson, a politician in York (present-day Toronto). Scott's Plains was renamed Peterborough in his honour. The Irish emigrated from the Emerald Isle to escape over-crowding, poverty, political unrest, religious tensions, disease and the potato famine. By 1851 almost half of the town of Peterborough claimed Irish ancestry. They cleared the land in the rolling hills of the Peterborough countryside.

In 1845, Sandford Fleming, inventor of Standard Time and designer of Canada's first postage stamp, moved to the city to live with Dr. John Hutchison and his family, staying until 1847. Dr. John Hutchison was one of Peterborough's first resident doctors.

Beginning in the late 1850s, a canoe building industry grew up in and around Peterborough. The Peterborough Canoe Company was founded in 1893, with the factory being built on the site of the original Adam Scott mill. From 1928–36 the Johnson Motor Company/Outboard Marine (the makers of motorized boat engines) was established as an outgrowth of the original industry.

Peterborough was one of the first places in the country to begin generating hydro electrical power (even before the plants at Niagara Falls). Companies like Edison General Electric Company (later Canadian General Electric) and America Cereal Company (later to become Quaker Oats, and in 2001 PepsiCo, Inc.), opened to take advantage of cheap hydro-electric power.

Table of Contents

Peterborough

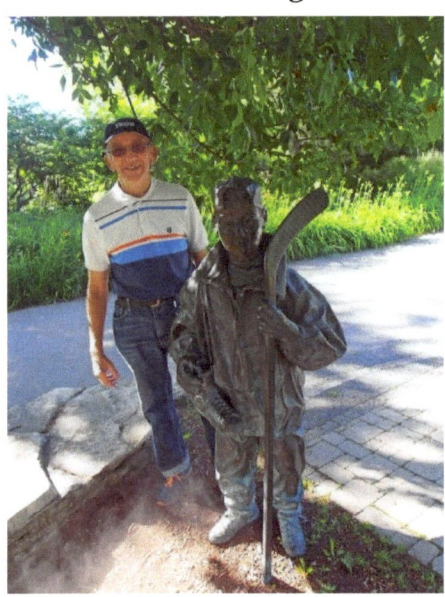

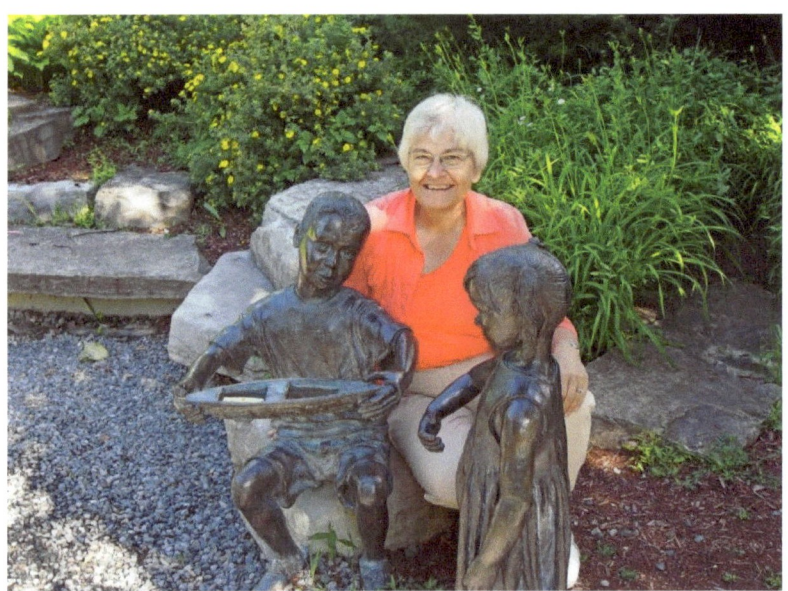

Boat Launching by Laura Brown Breetvelt

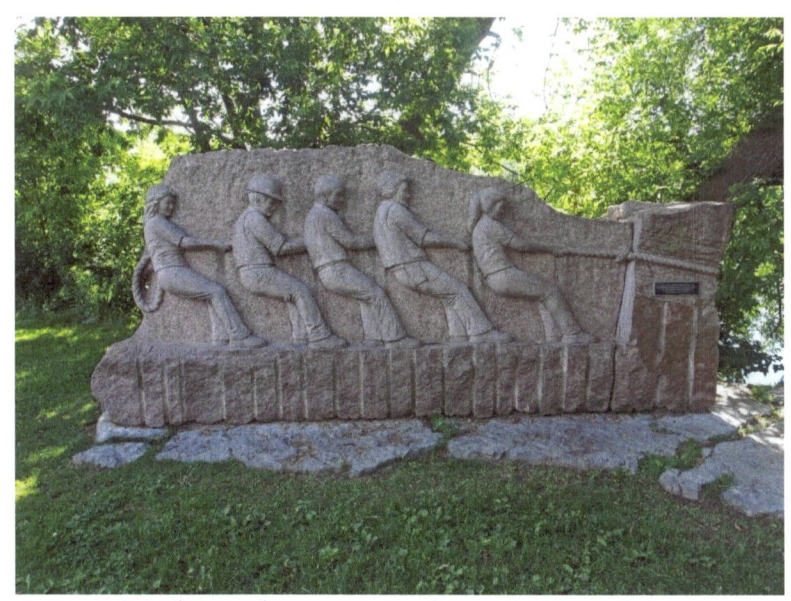

Dedicated to men and women workers
past, present and future

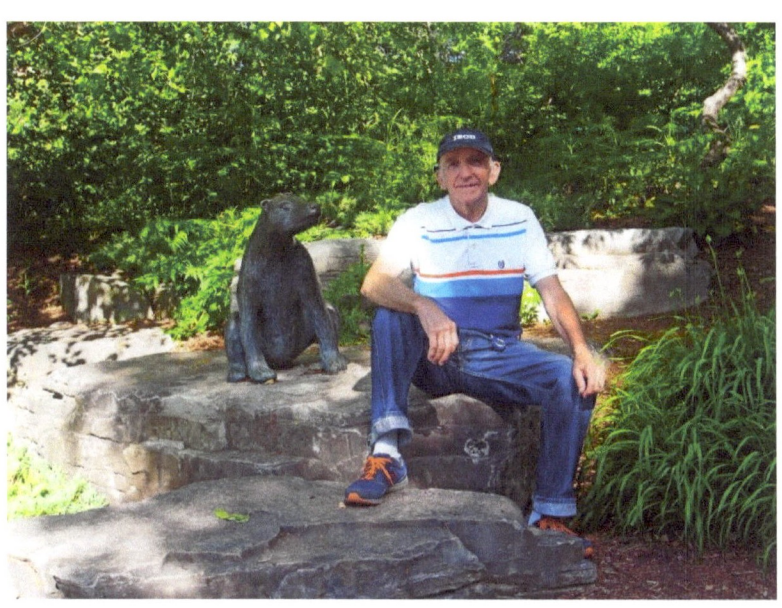

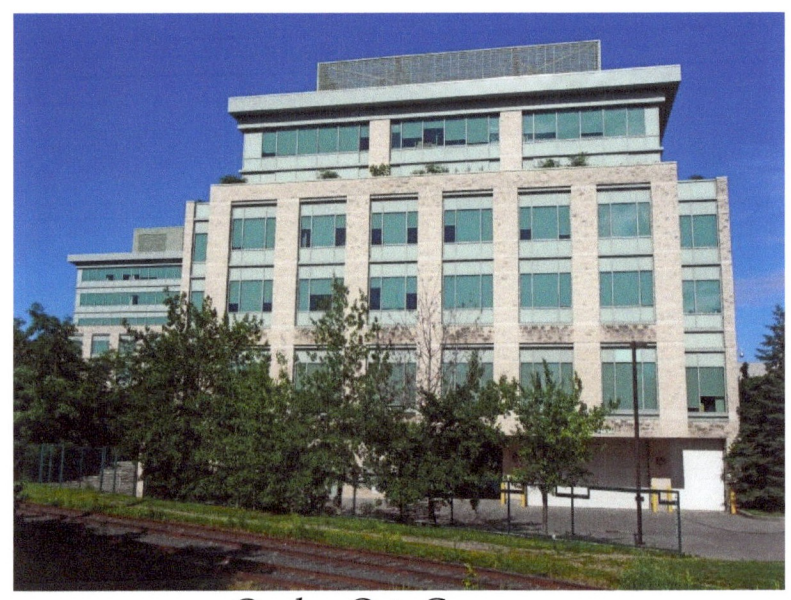

Quaker Oats Company

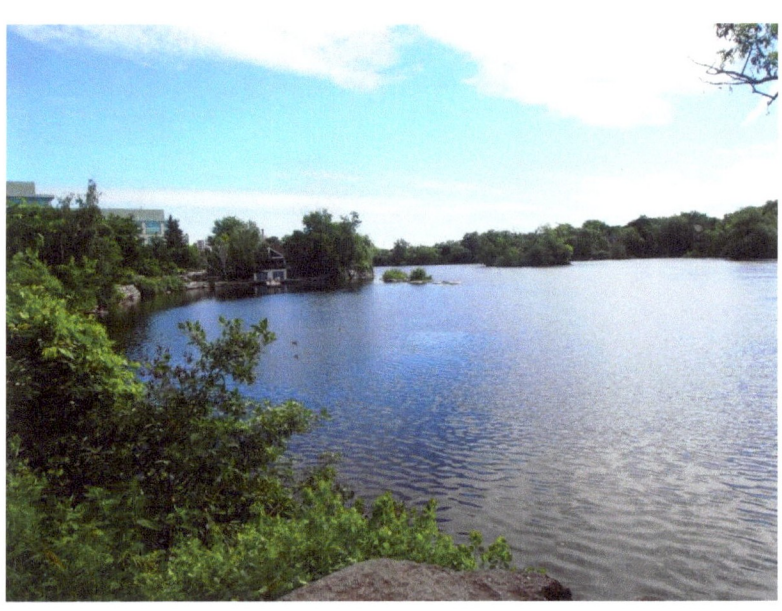

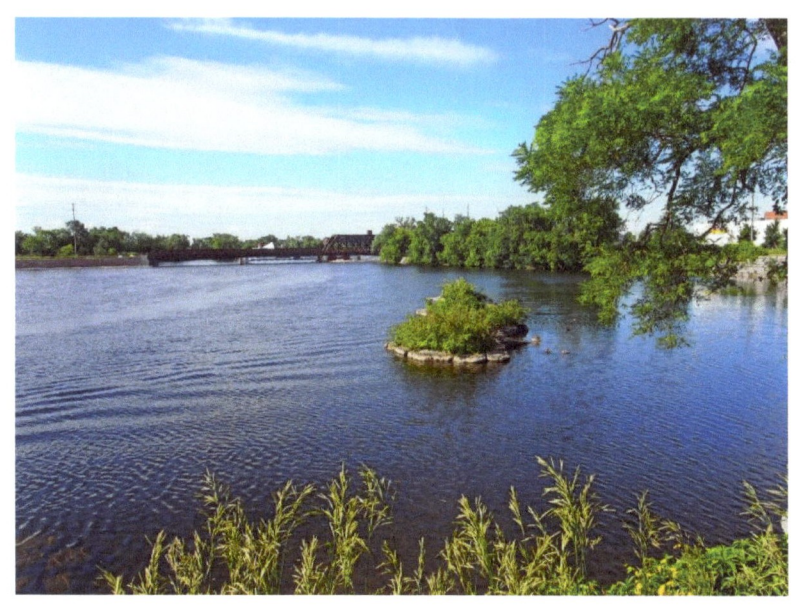

Otonabee River

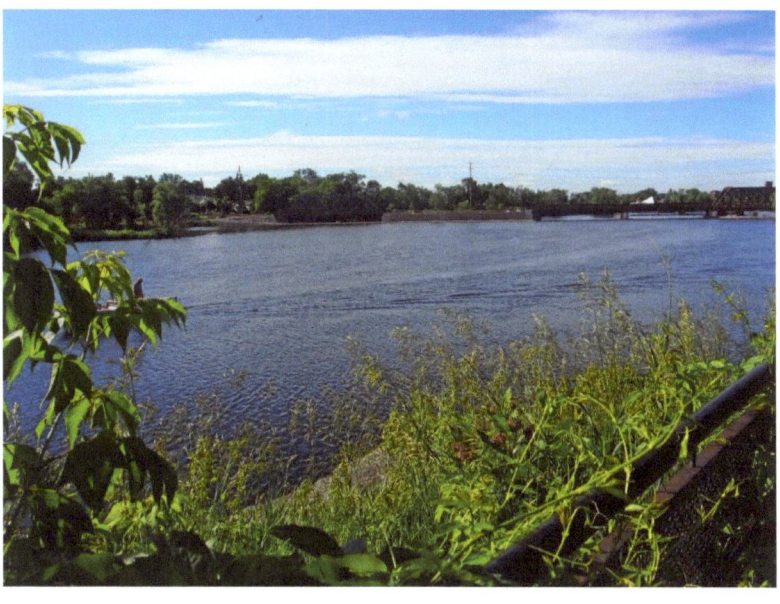

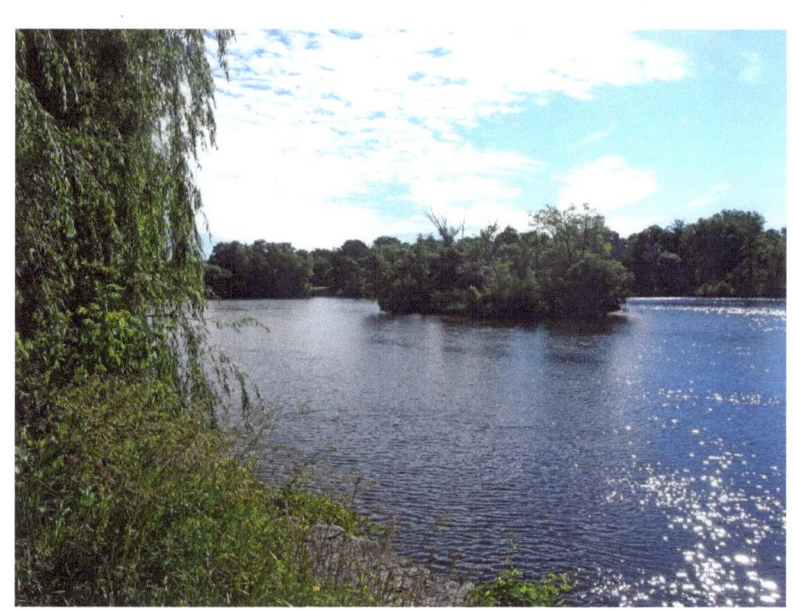

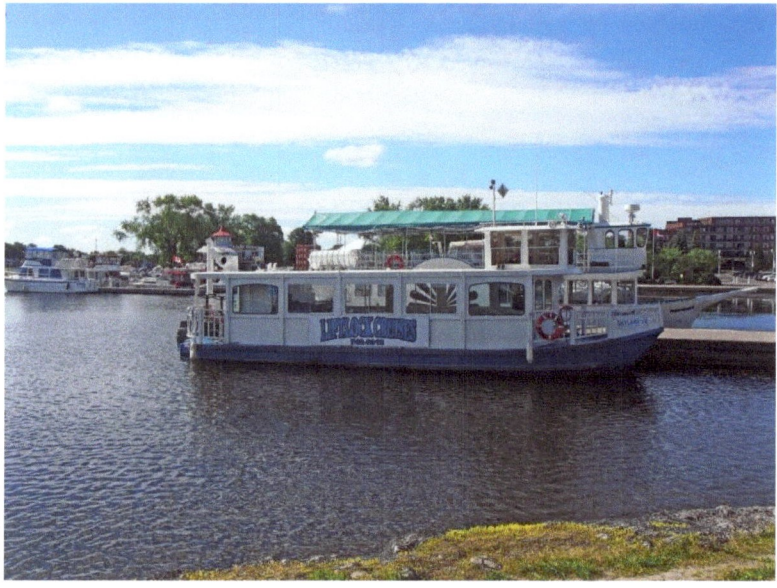

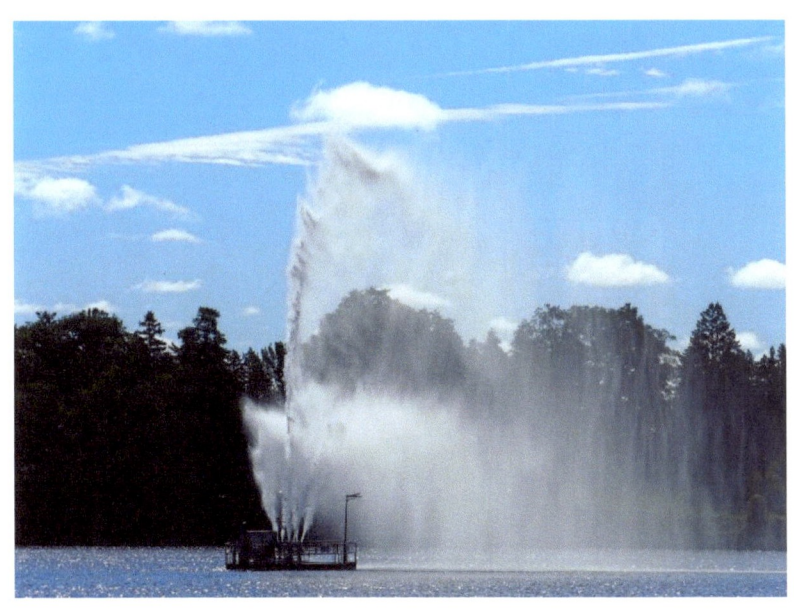

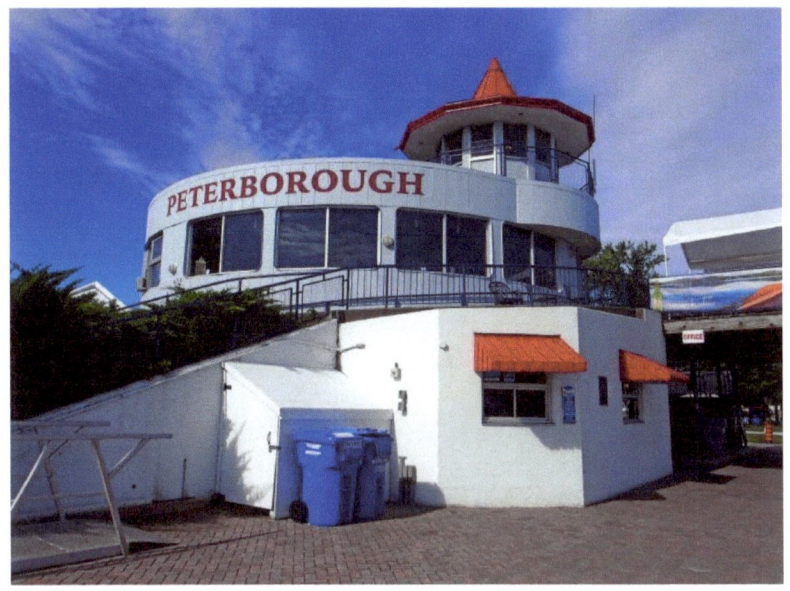

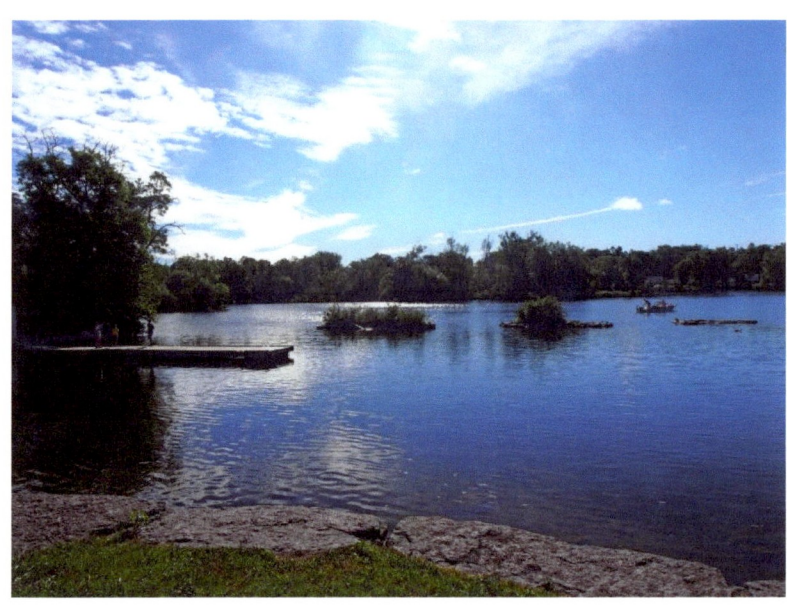

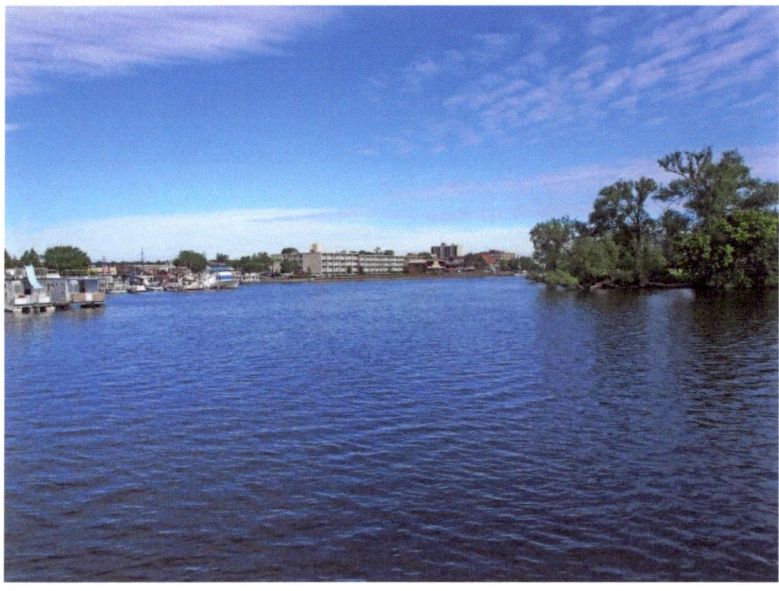

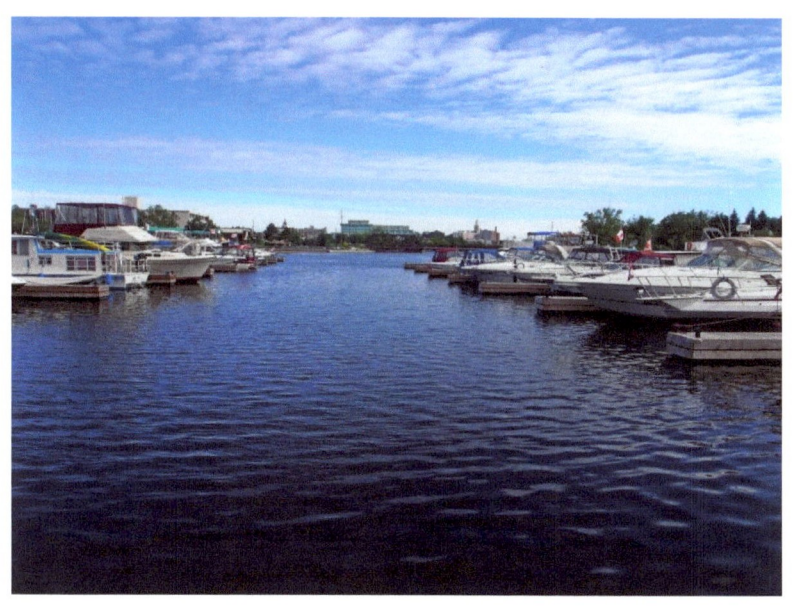

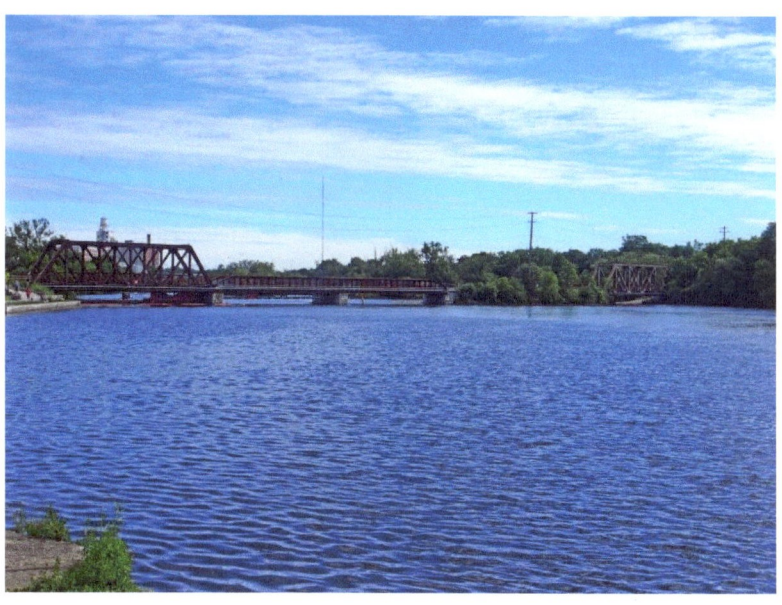

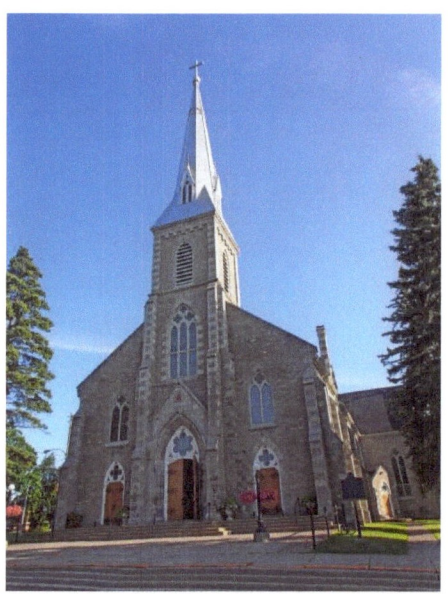

411 Reid Street - The Cathedral of St. Peter in Chains established in 1826 to serve the large Irish Catholic population of the surrounding Robinson settlement. This building erected in 1837-38 of stone from nearby Jackson's Creek is one of the oldest remaining Catholic churches in Ontario. It follows the modified Gothic Revival style popular in Upper Canada during the period. In 1882 when the Diocese of Peterborough was created, St. Peter's became a cathedral. Although altered on various occasions, St. Peter's-in-Chains has retained its original elegance and imposing form.

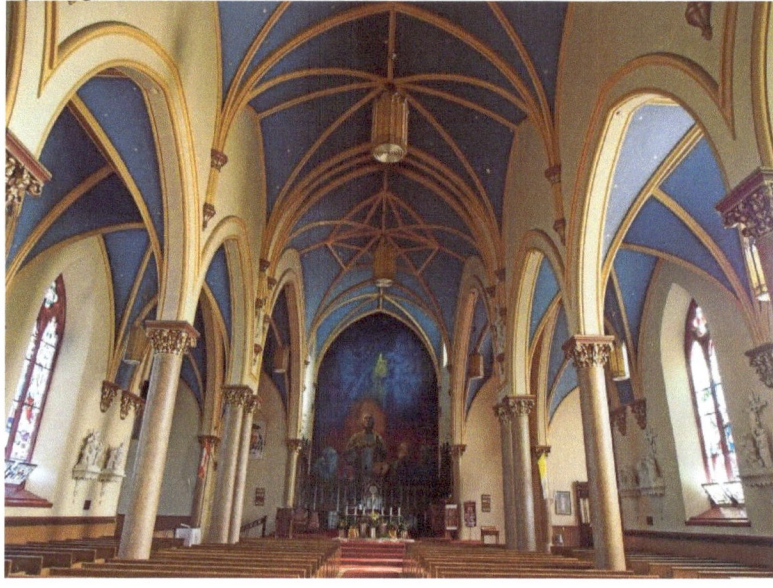

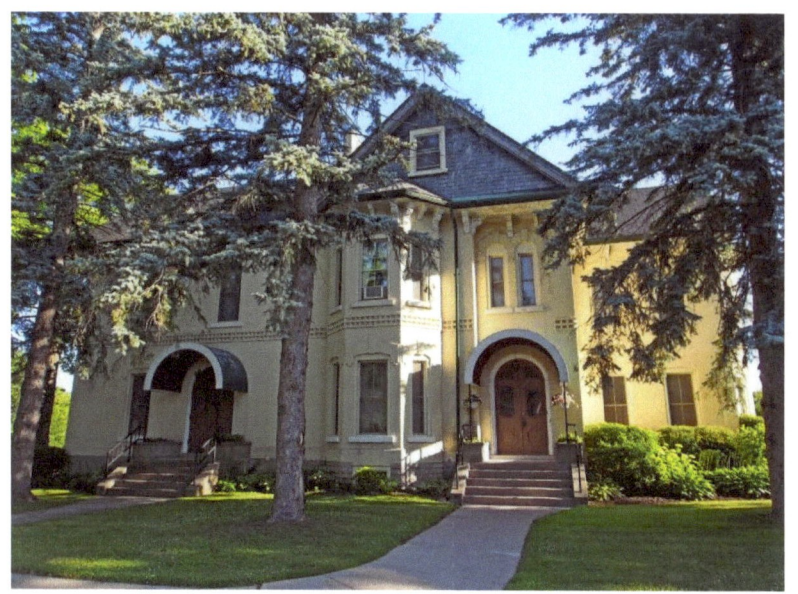

Reid Street – Gothic, cornice brackets

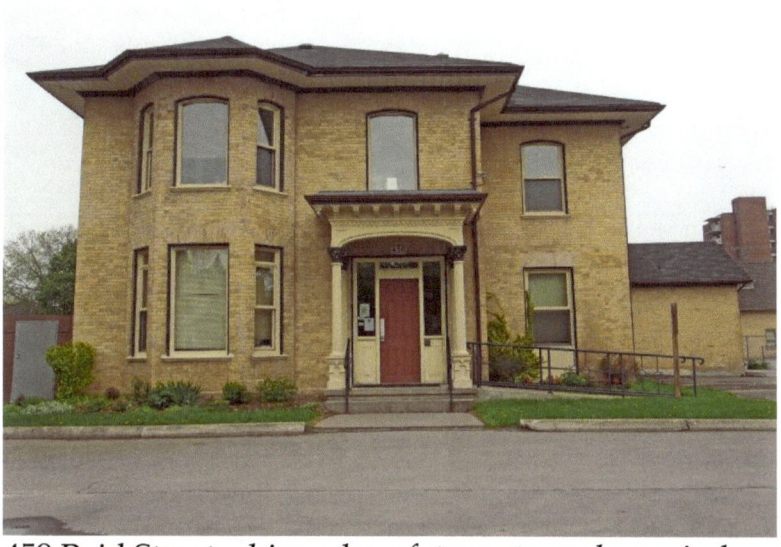

459 Reid Street – hipped roof, two-storey bay window

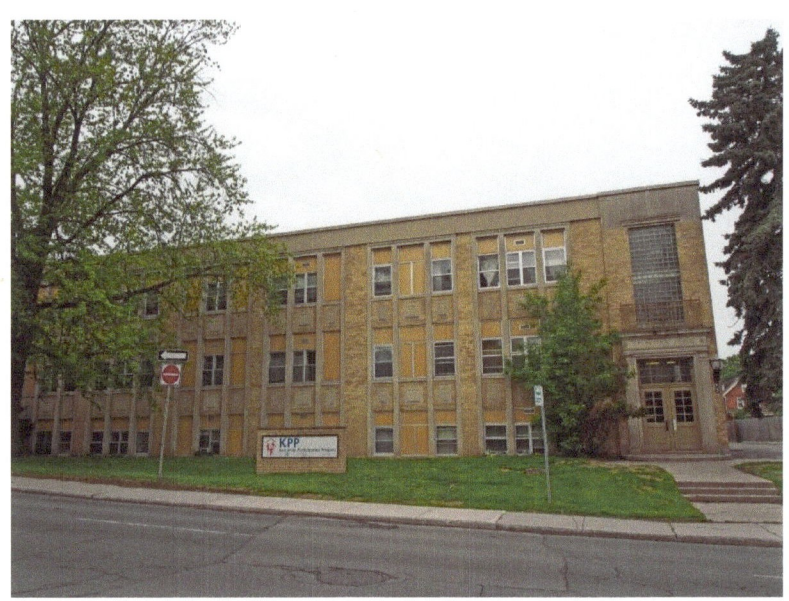

443 Reid Street – St. Peter's School

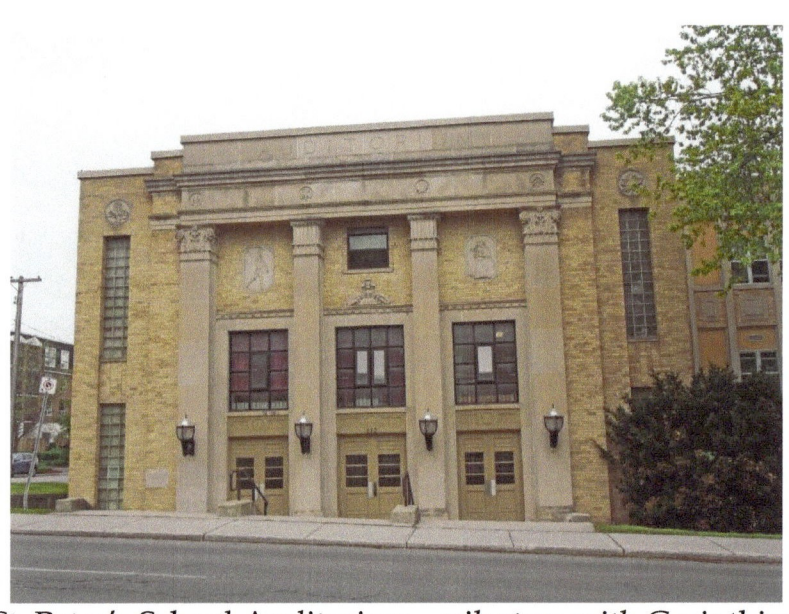

St. Peter's School Auditorium – pilasters with Corinthian capitals

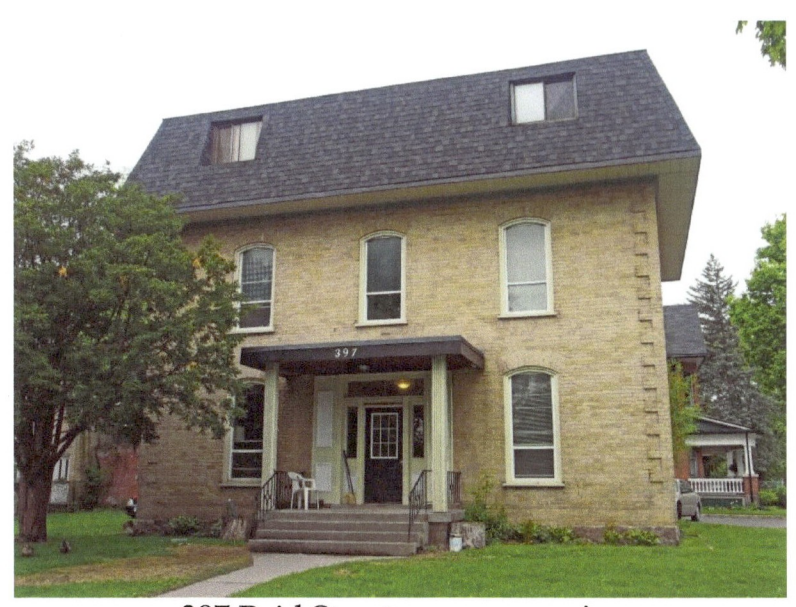

397 Reid Street – corner quoins

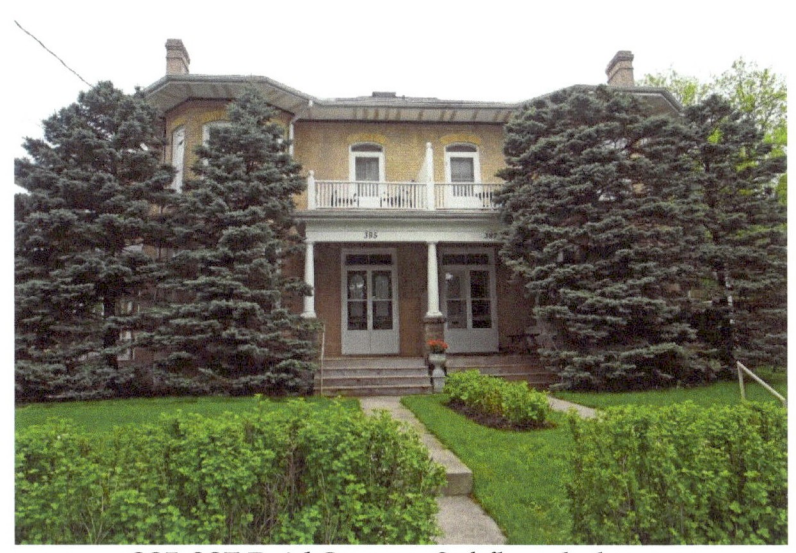

385-387 Reid Street – 2nd floor balcony

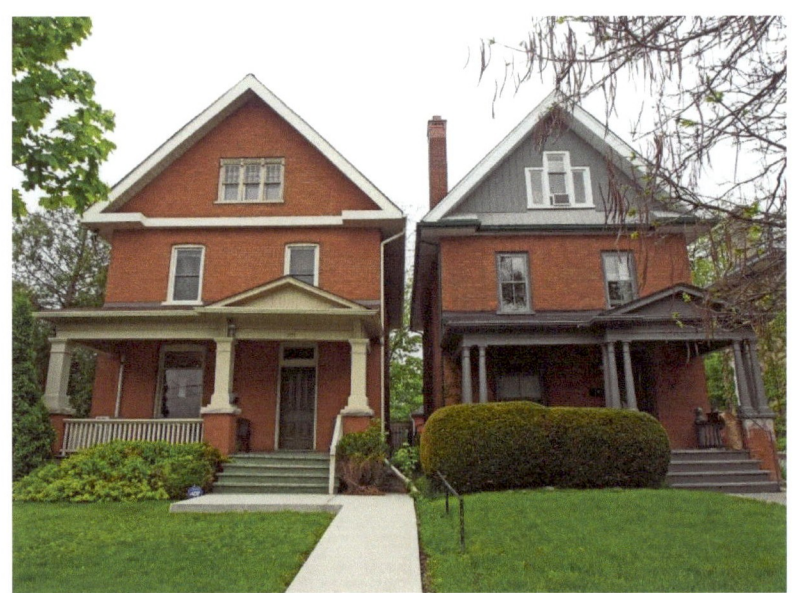

377 Reid Street
Cornice return, pediment

379 Reid Street
Palladian window
pediment

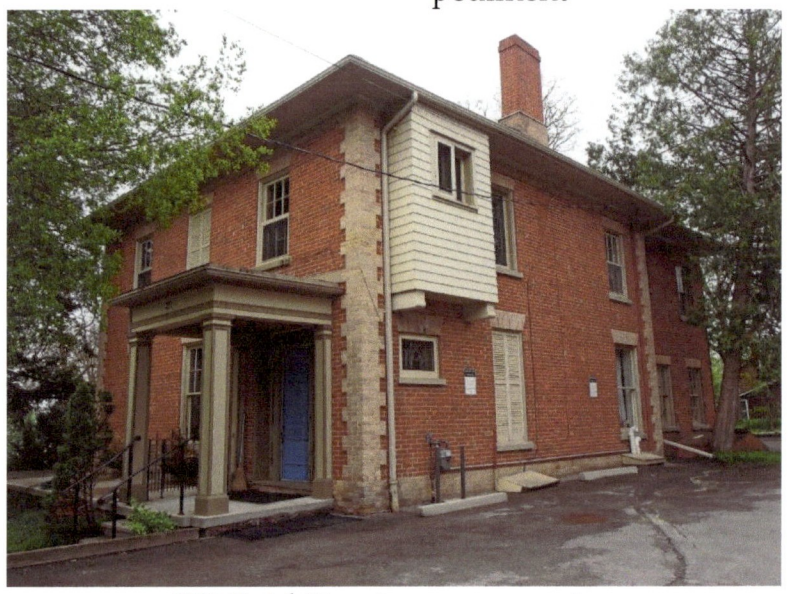

371 Reid Street – corner quoins

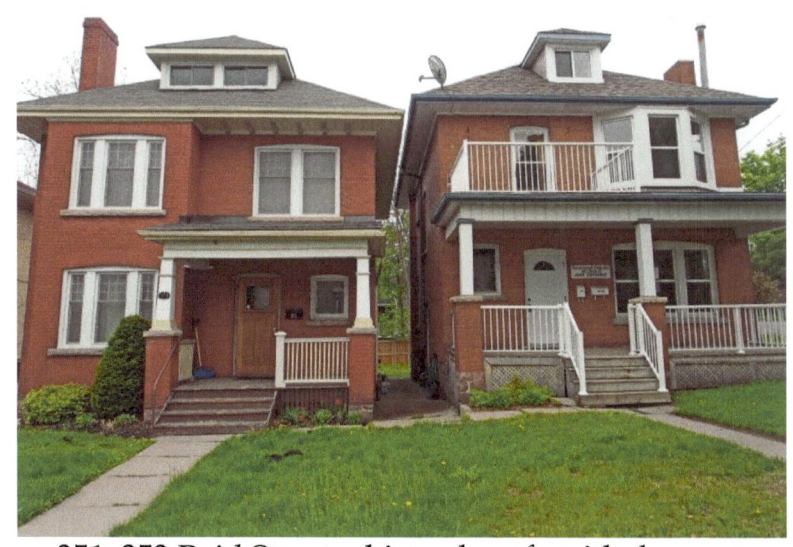

351, 353 Reid Street – hipped roofs with dormers
2nd floor balcony
Bay window

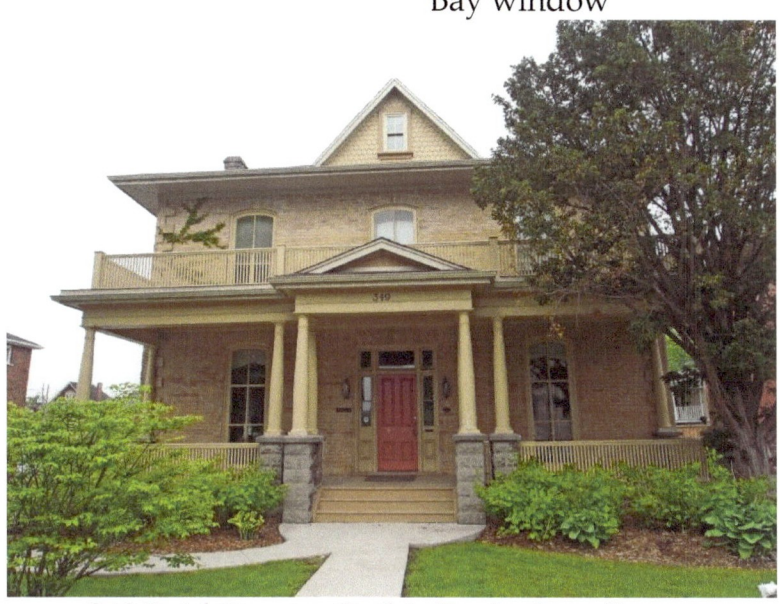

349 Reid Street – Gothic Revival, pediment

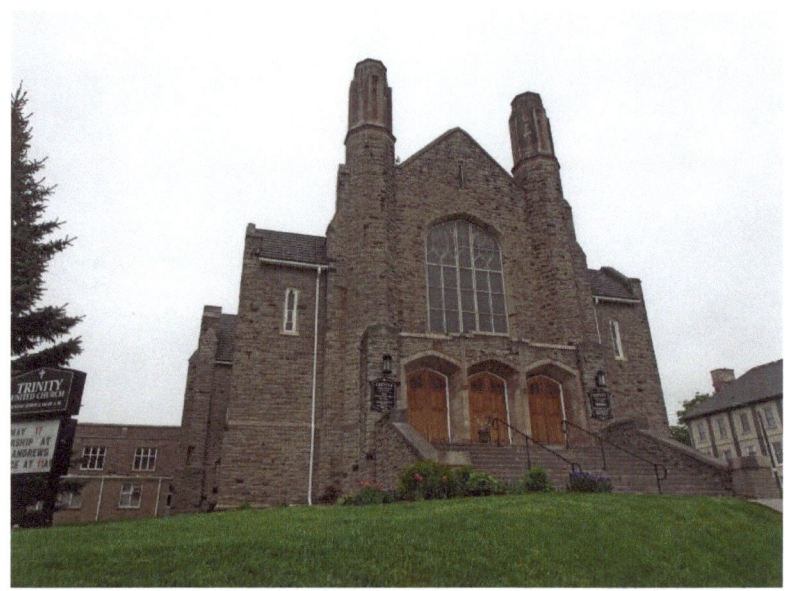

360 Reid Street – Trinity United Church started as the Charlotte Street Wesleyan Methodist Mission on Charlotte Street, south of the present site, in 1872, with the name changed to the Charlotte Street Methodist Church in 1884. From 1914-1916, a new church was built on a nearby site with the name changed to Trinity United in 1925.

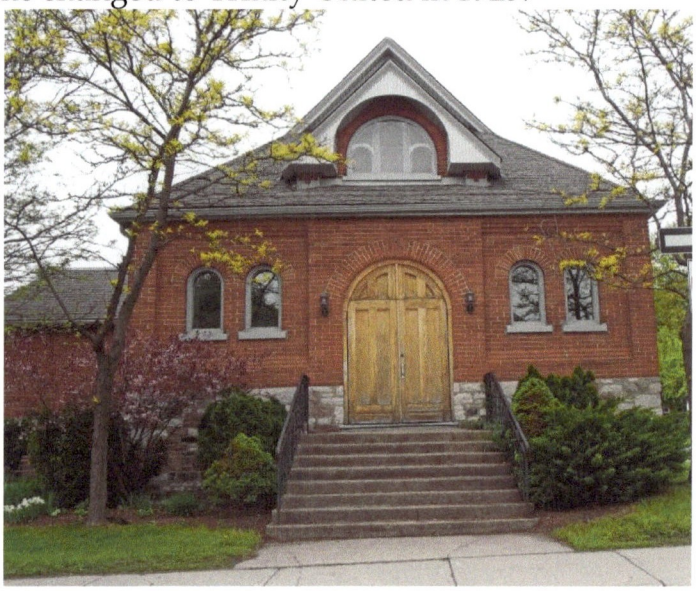

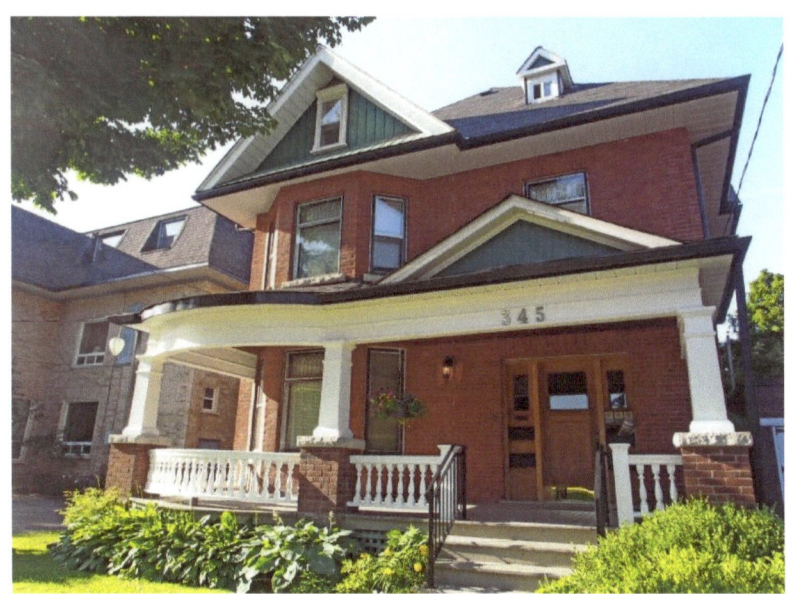

345 Hunter Street West – Edwardian, small dormer in attic, pediment

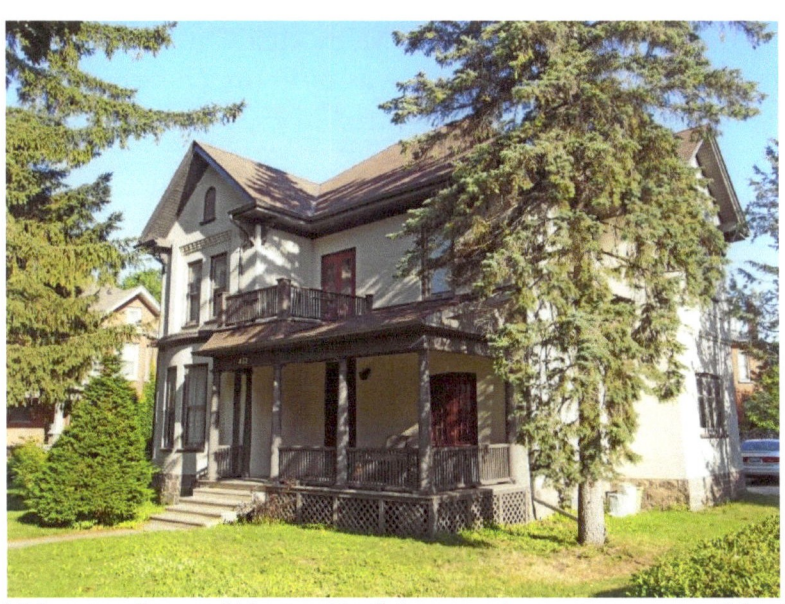

452 Hunter Street West – Gothic, cornice return on gable, 2nd floor balcony

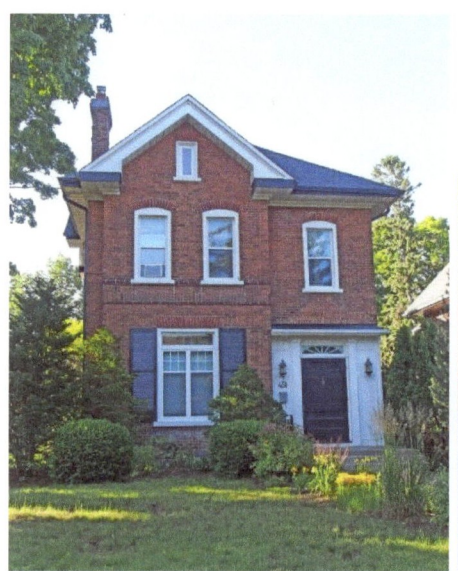

451 Hunter Street West
Gothic

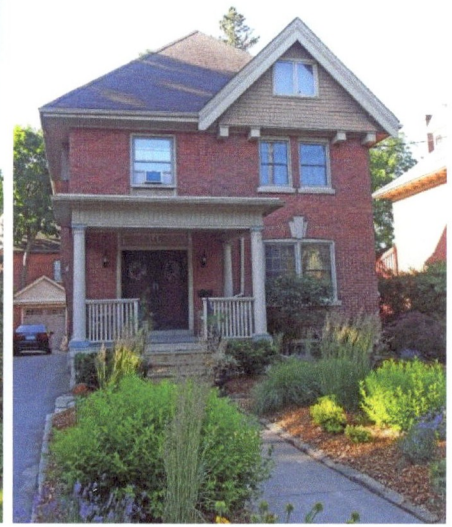

455 Hunter Street West
Edwardian

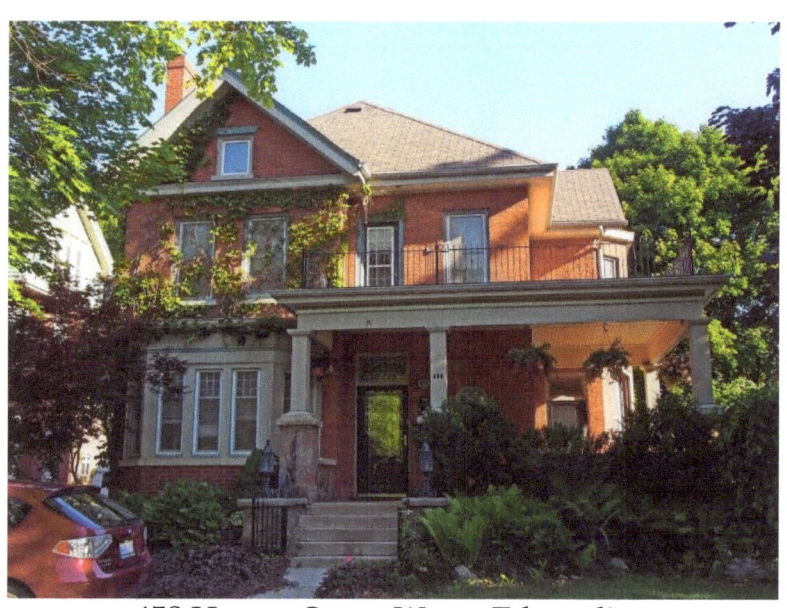

458 Hunter Street West - Edwardian

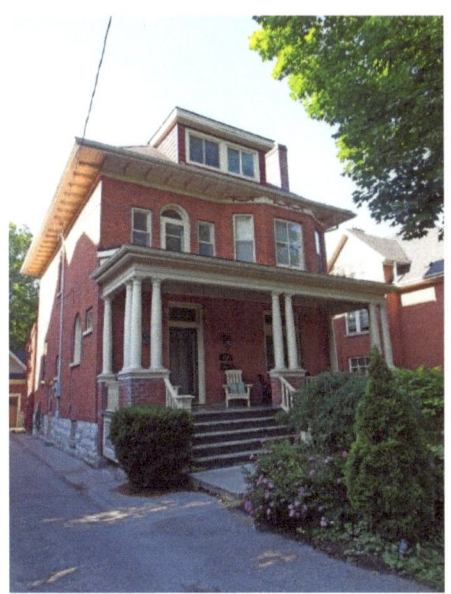 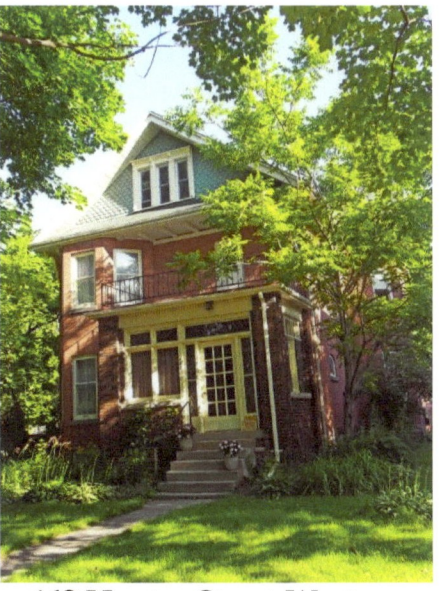

459 Hunter Street West
Italianate, dormer

462 Hunter Street West
Edwardian

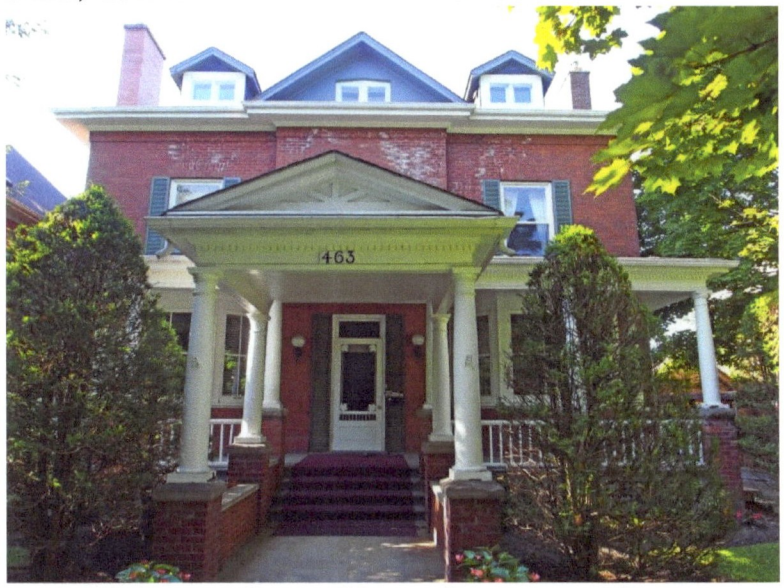

463 Hunter Street West – dormers, pediment

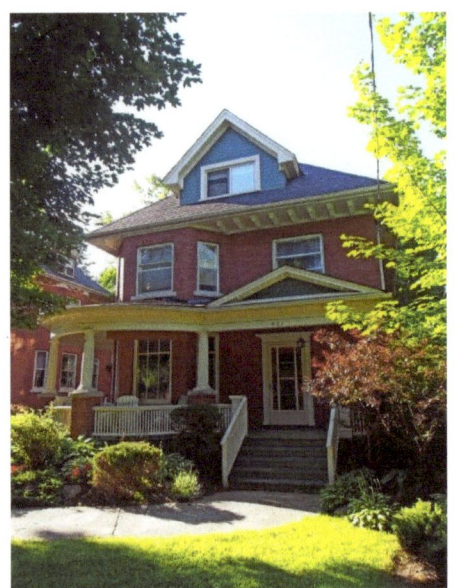

461 Hunter Street West - dormer

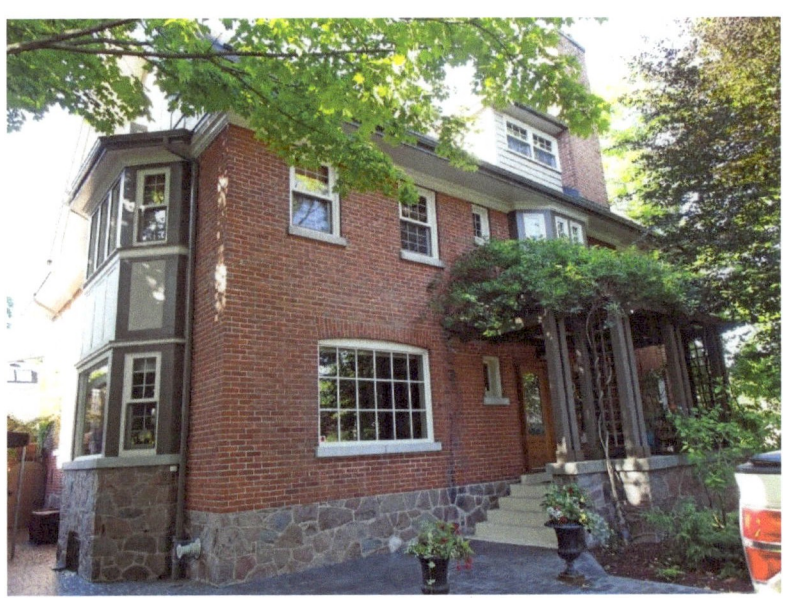

475 Hunter Street West

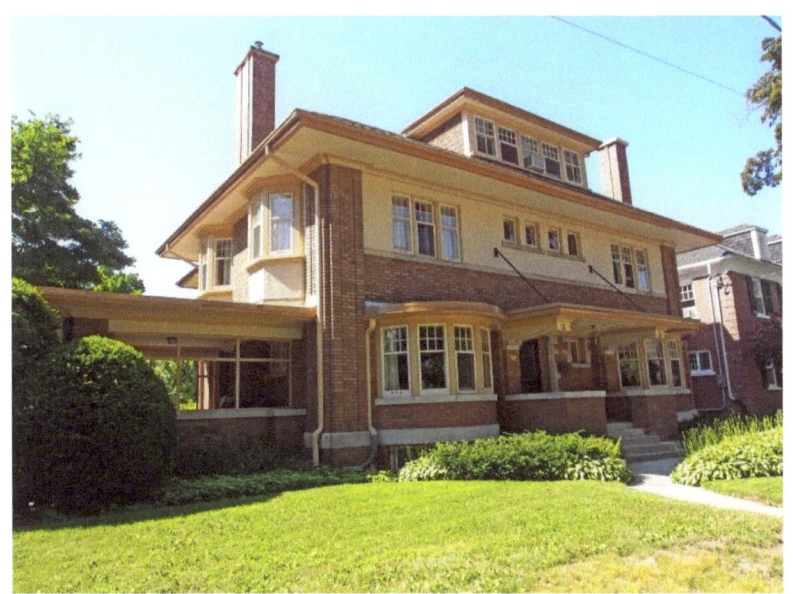

487 Hunter Street West - dormer

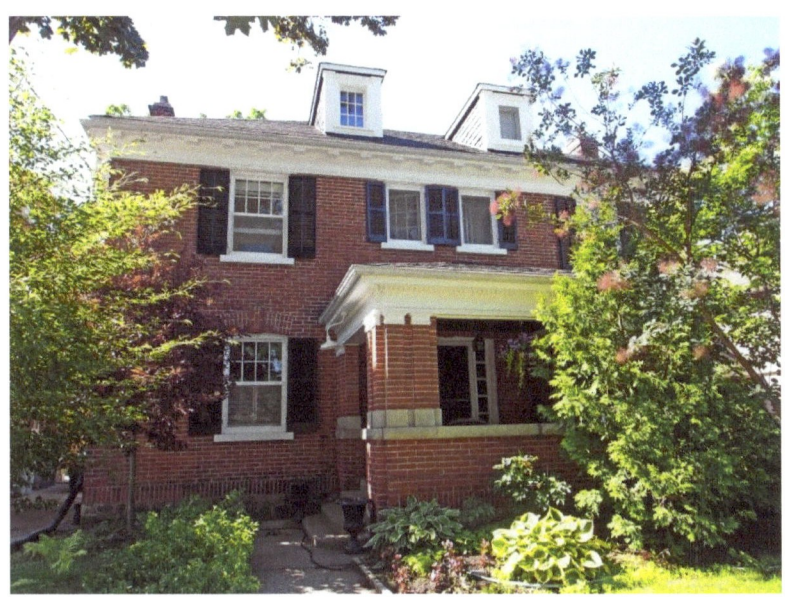

491 Hunter Street West – dormers in attic

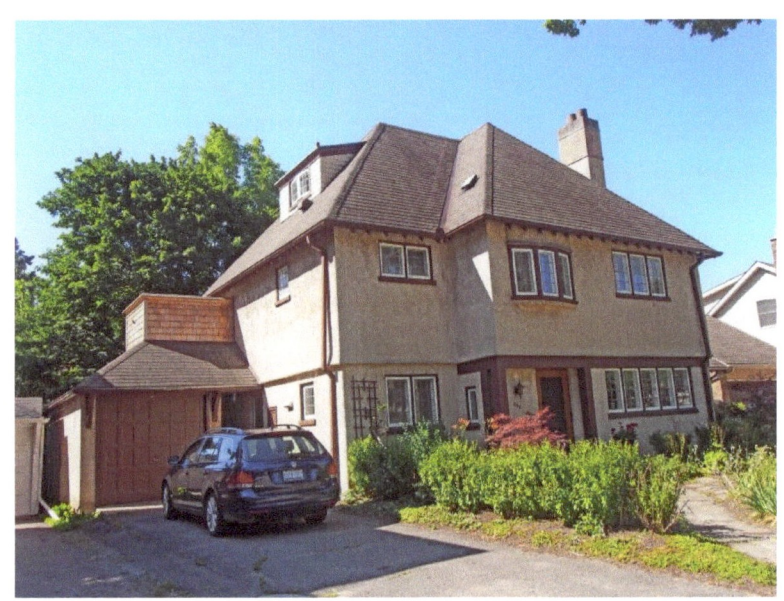

493 Hunter Street West

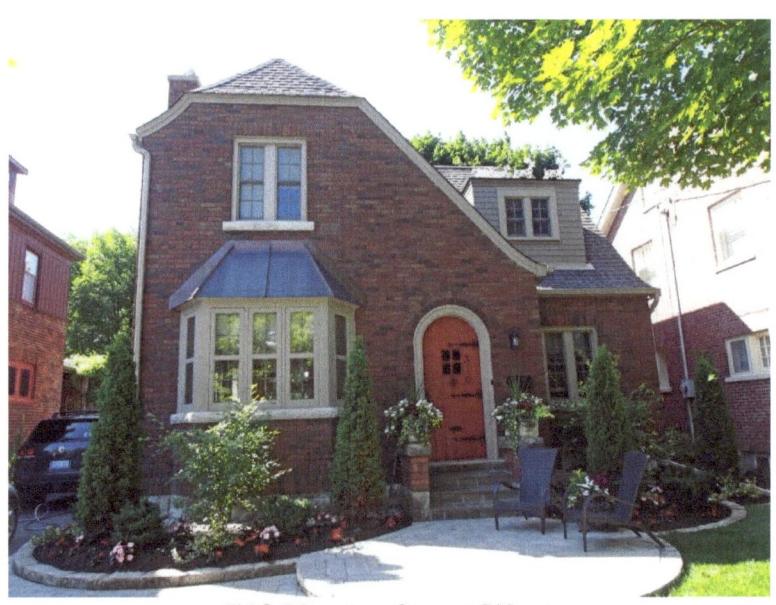

519 Hunter Street West

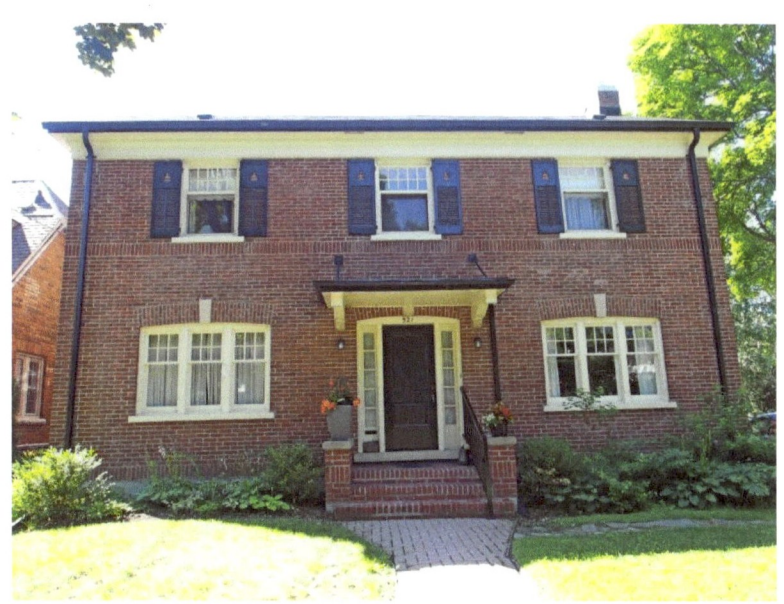

521 Hunter Street West - Italianate

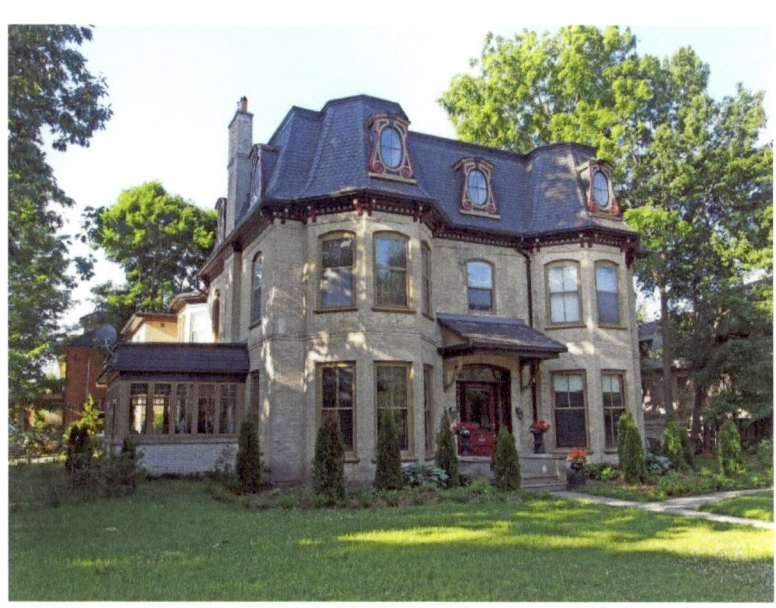

359 Downie Street – Second Empire style, mansard roof, window hoods, 2 storey bay windows

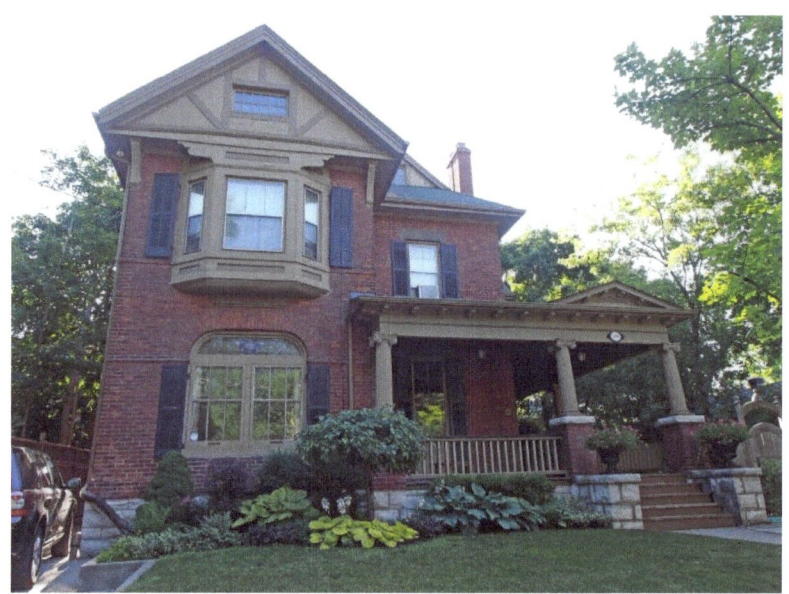

396 Downie Street – Tudor, bay window, Ionic capitals

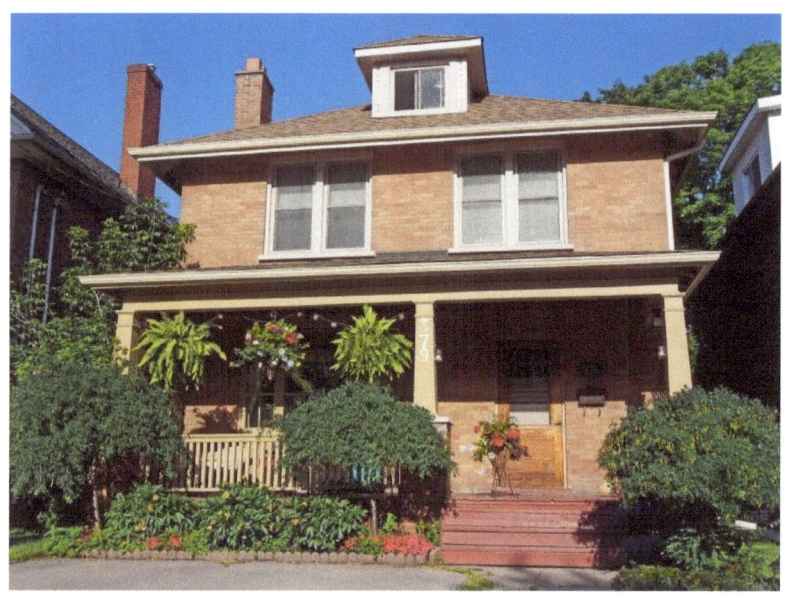

379 Downie Street – Italianate, hipped roof, dormer

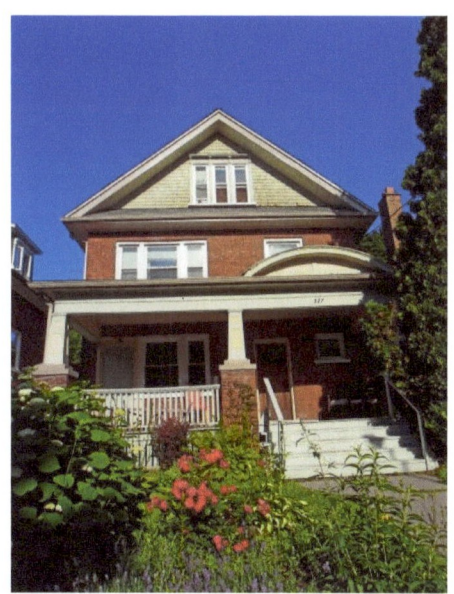

377 Downie Street - Edwardian

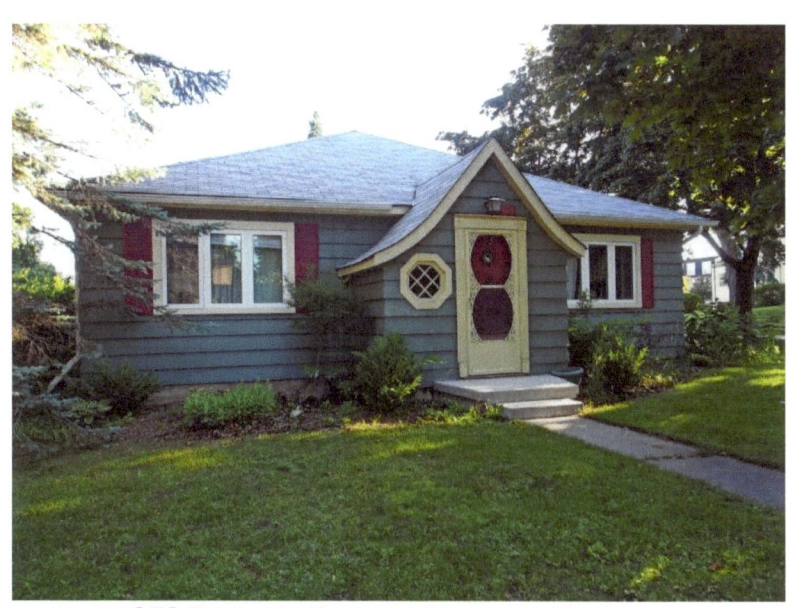

358 Downie Street – Regency Cottage

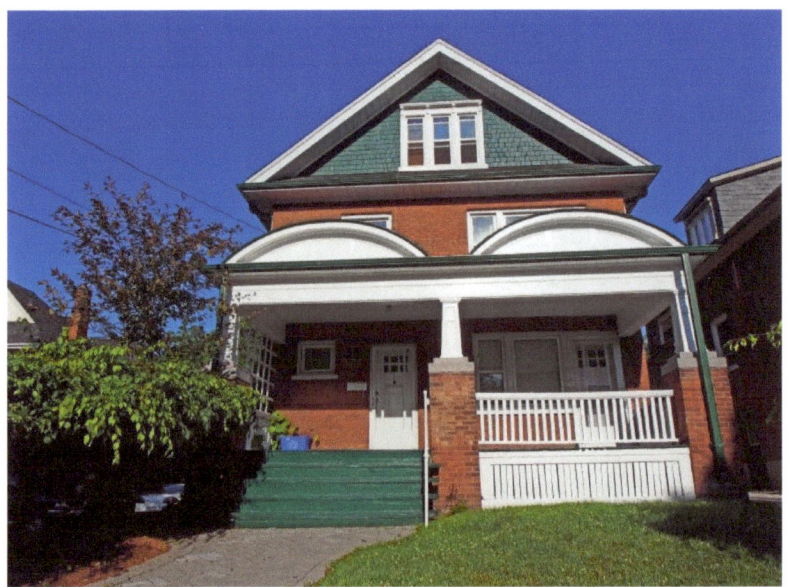

375 Downie Street - Edwardian

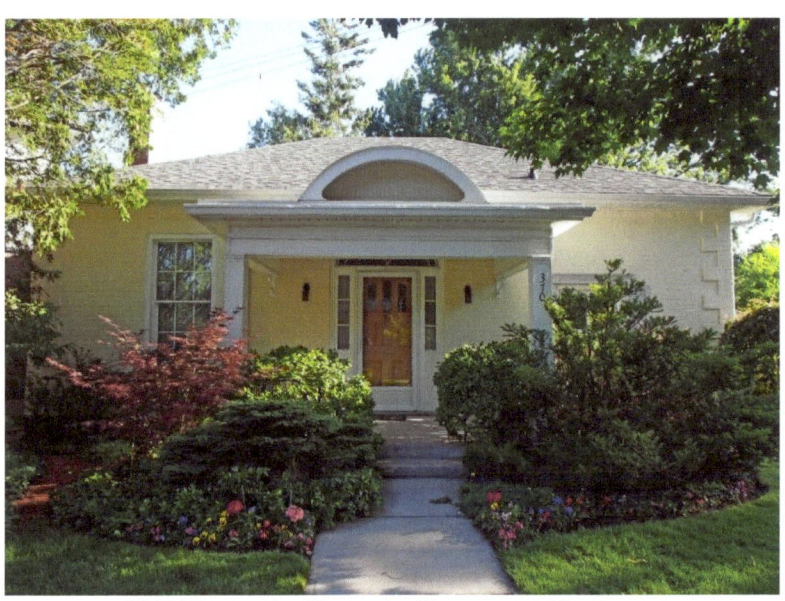

370 Downie Street – Regency Cottage

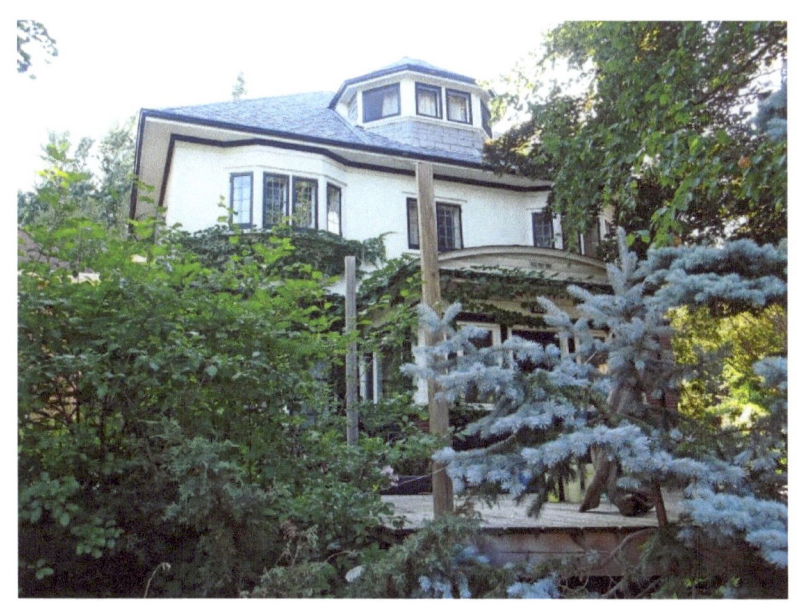

374 Downie Street – dormer in attic, hipped roof

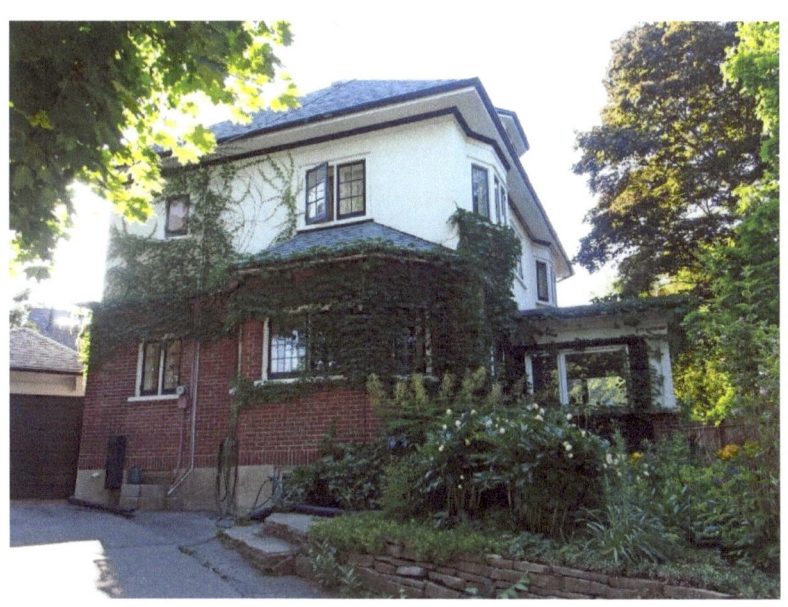

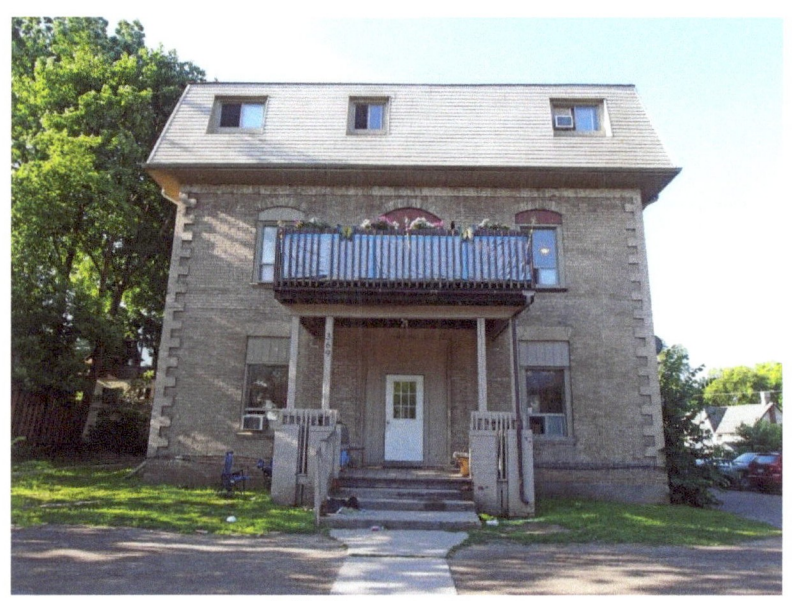

369 Downie Street

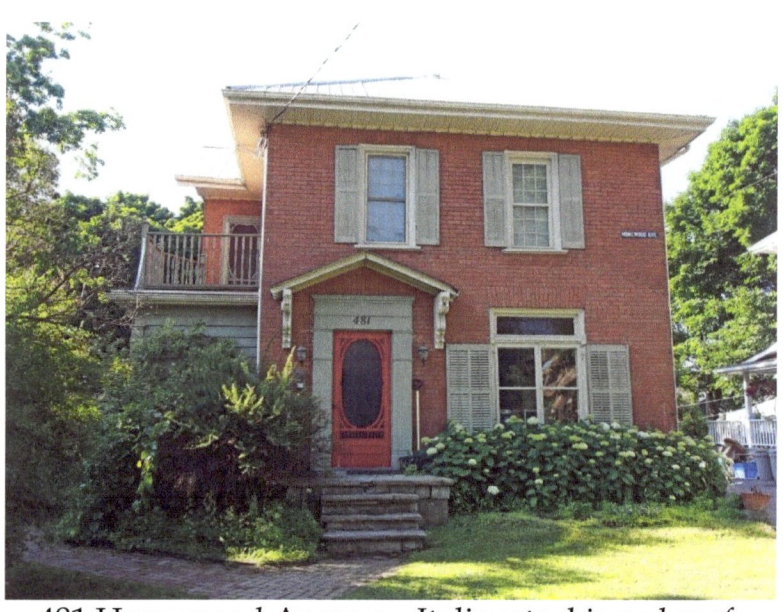

481 Homewood Avenue – Italianate, hipped roof,
2nd floor balcony

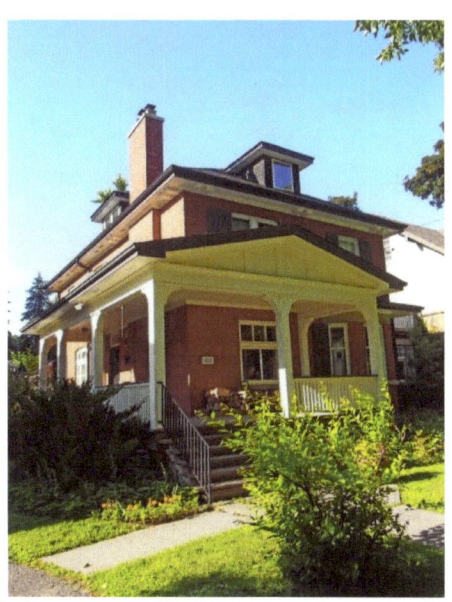

491 Homewood Avenue – Italianate, dormer in attic, pediment

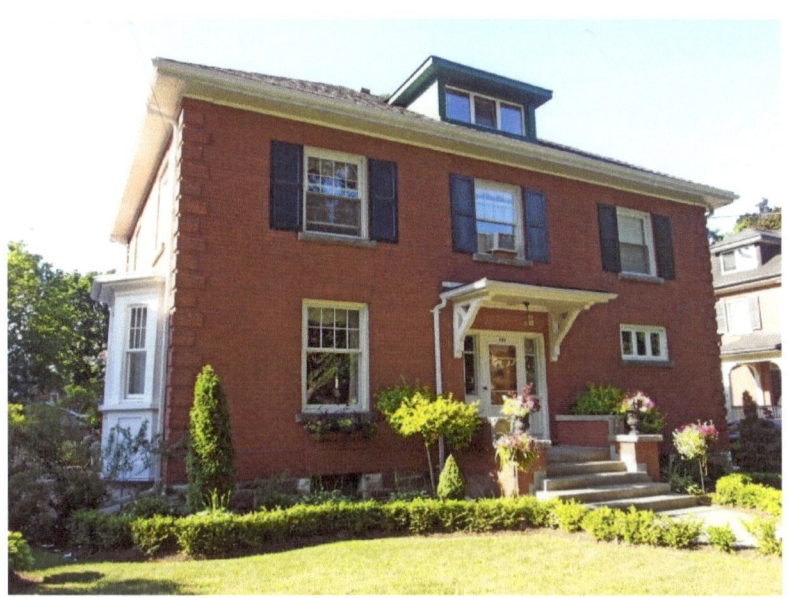

483 Homewood Avenue – Italianate, dormer

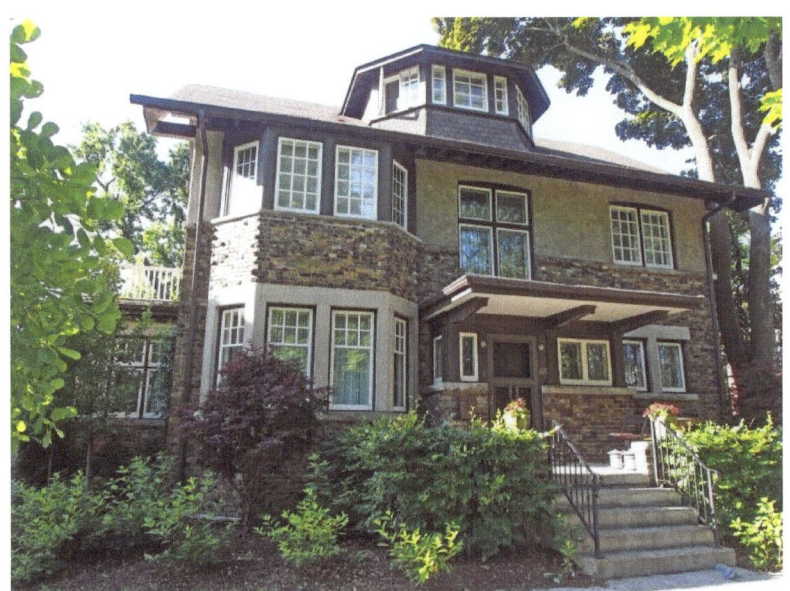

499 Homewood Avenue – belvedere on roof

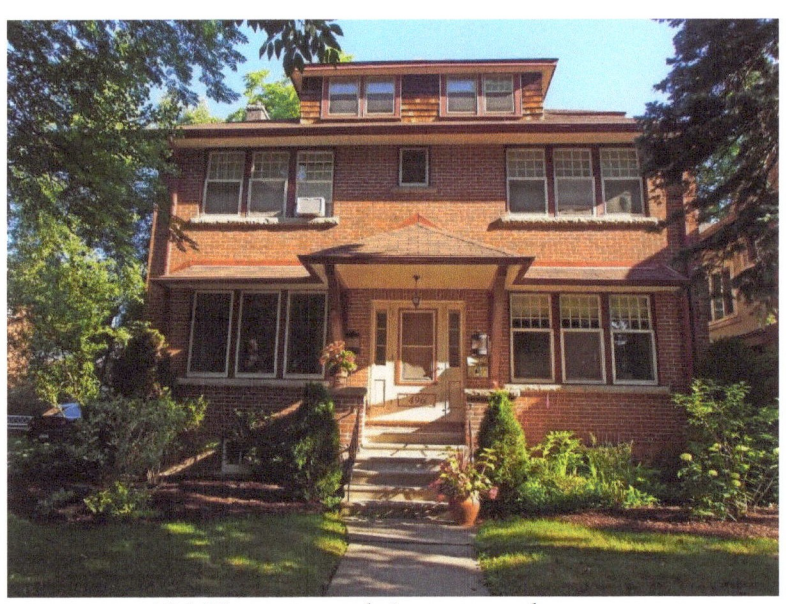

496 Homewood Avenue - dormers

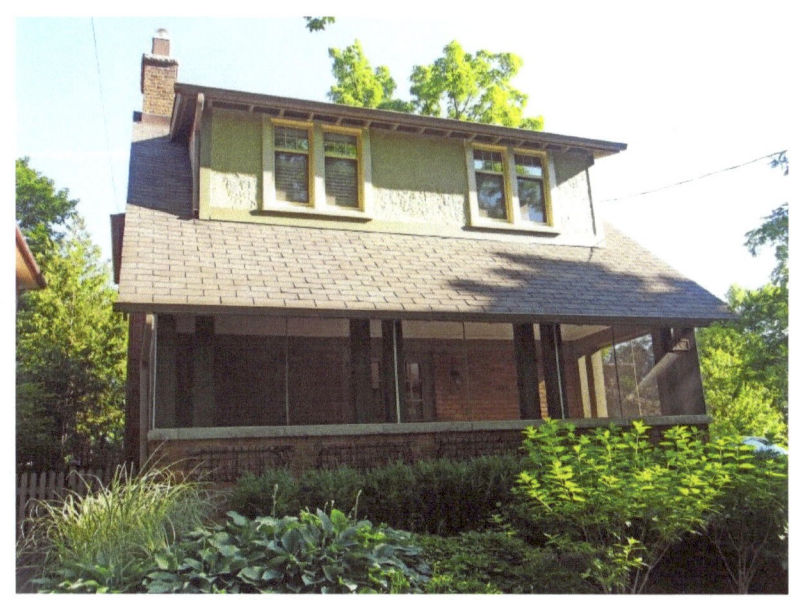

492 Homewood Avenue

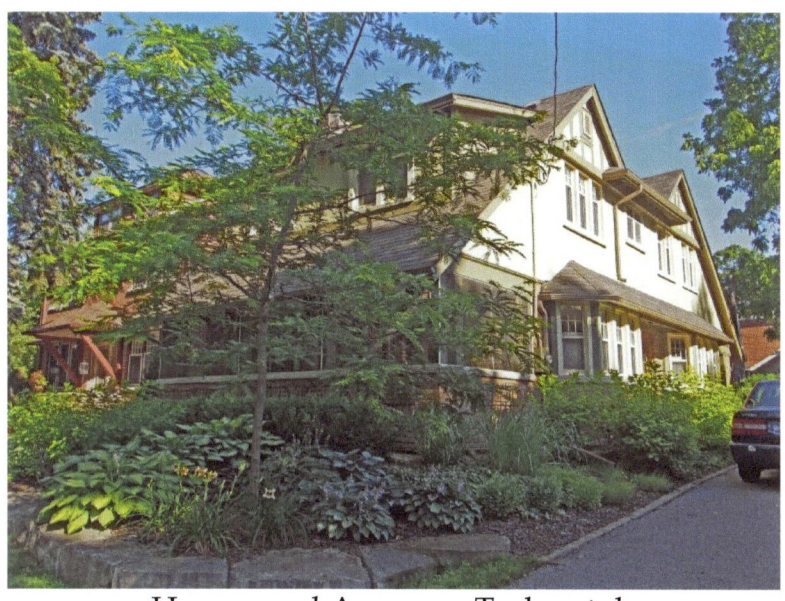

Homewood Avenue – Tudor style

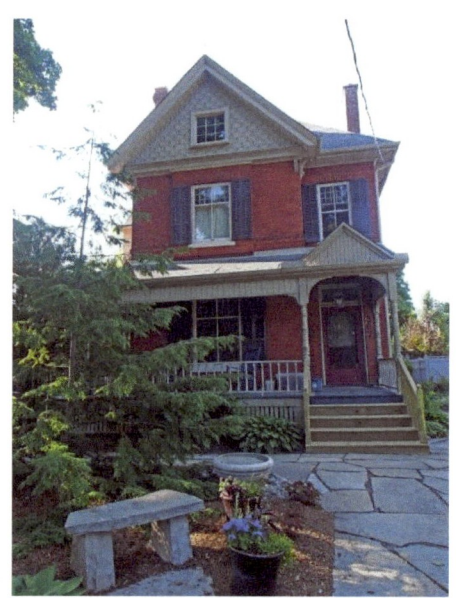

507 Homewood Avenue - Edwardian

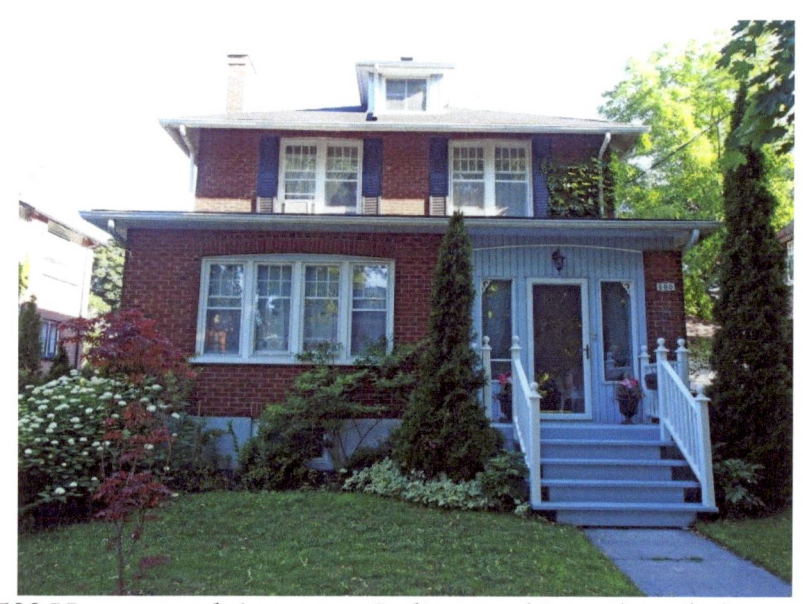

500 Homewood Avenue – Italianate, hipped roof, dormer

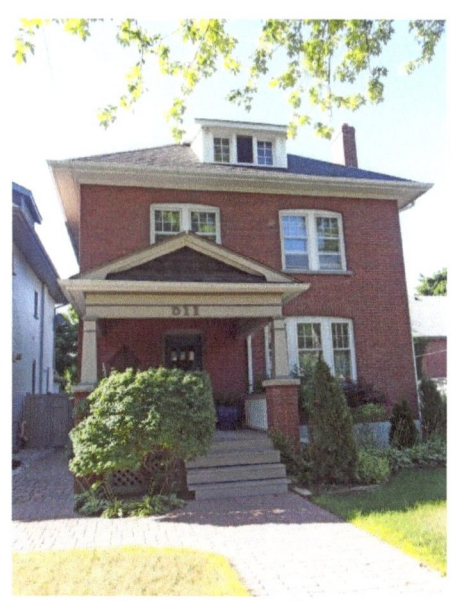

511 Homewood Avenue – dormer, pediment

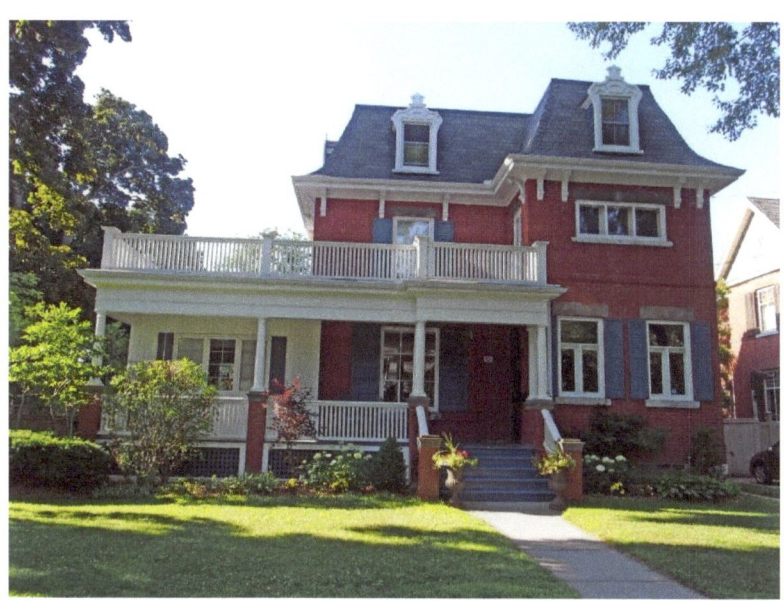

503 Homewood Avenue – Second Empire, mansard roof, dormers with window hoods, 2nd floor verandah

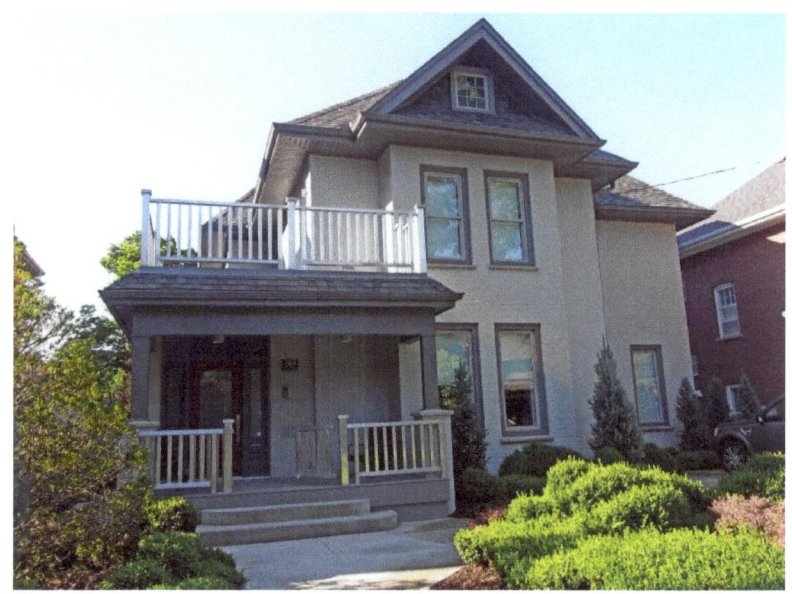

509 Homewood Avenue – Edwardian, 2nd floor balcony

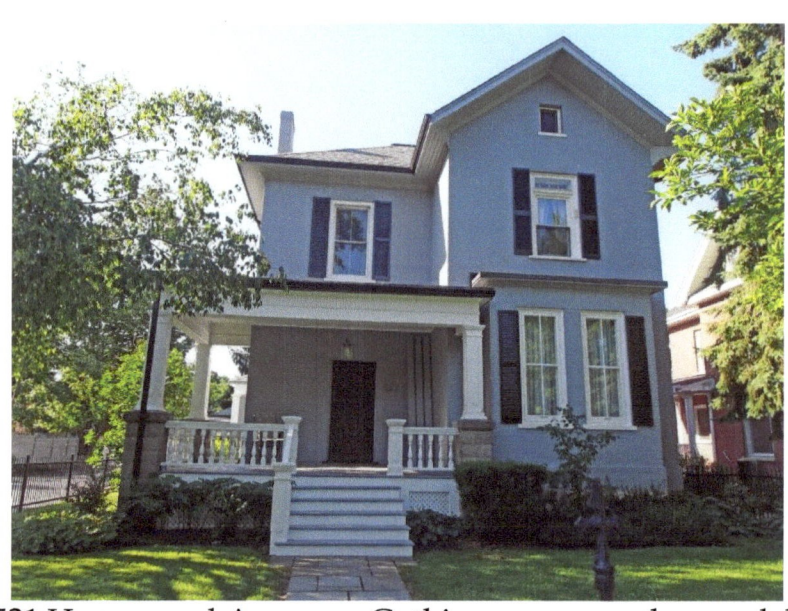

521 Homewood Avenue – Gothic, wraparound verandah

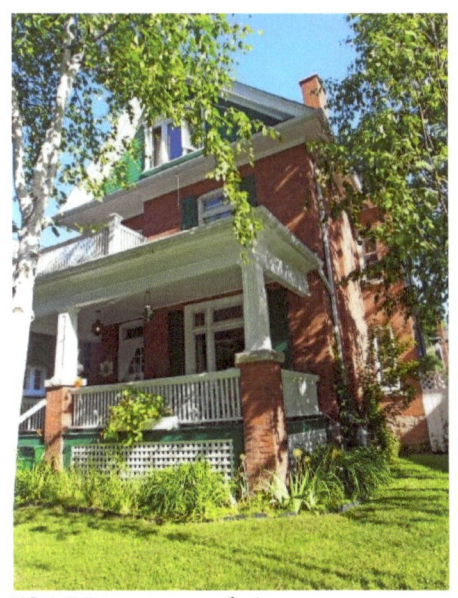

524 Homewood Avenue   529 Homewood Avenue
Edwardian

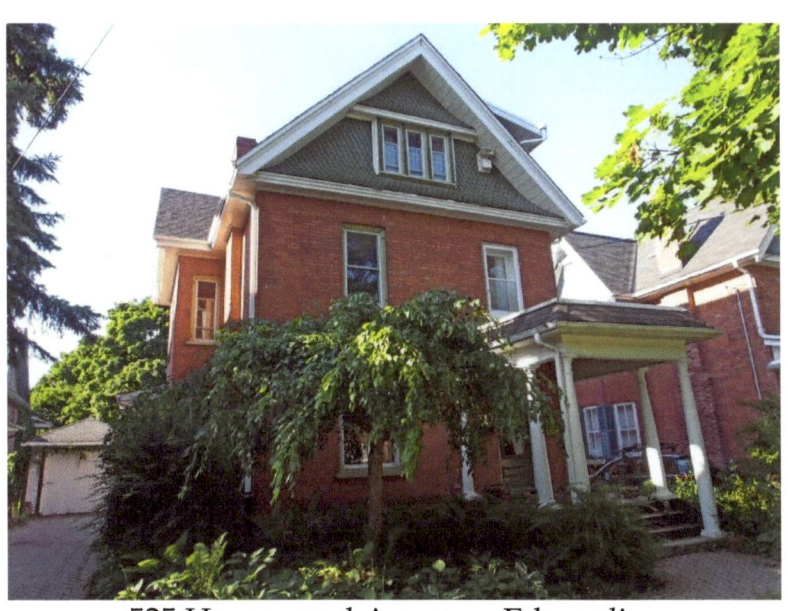

525 Homewood Avenue - Edwardian

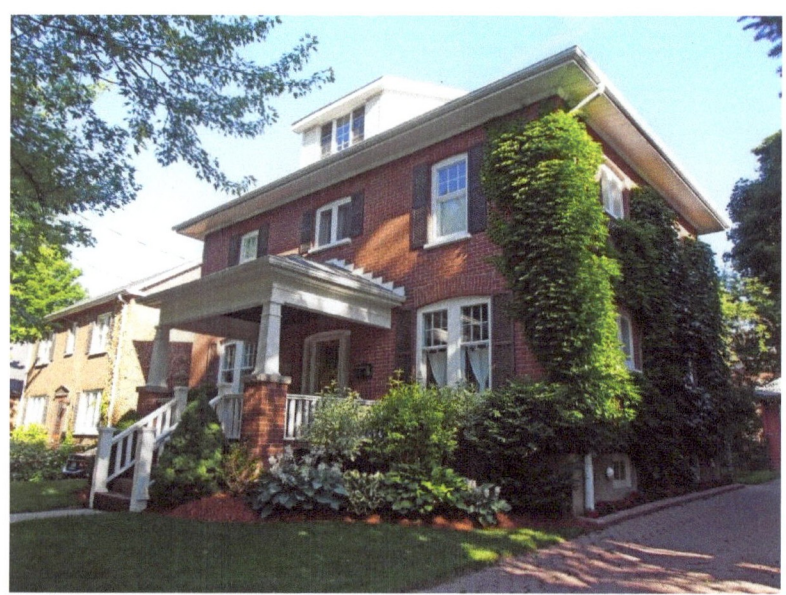

526 Homewood Avenue – Italianate, dormer

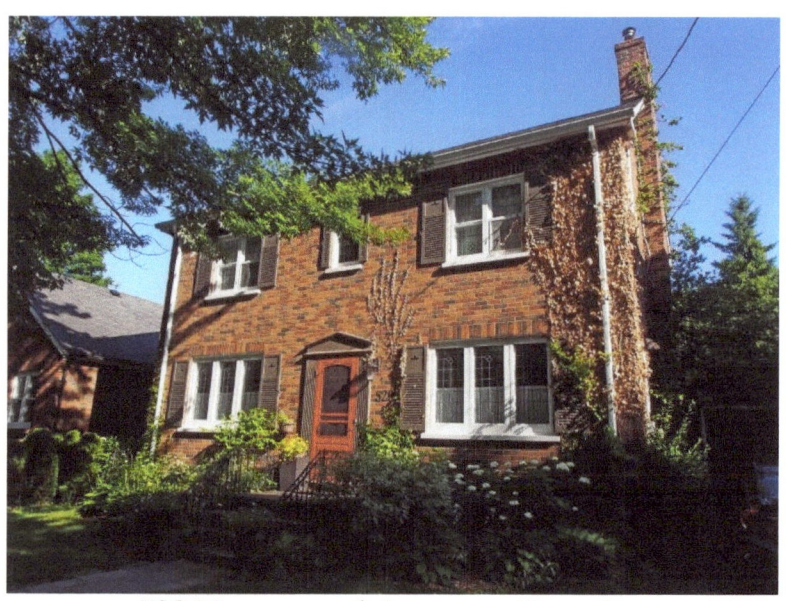

528 Homewood Avenue - Georgian

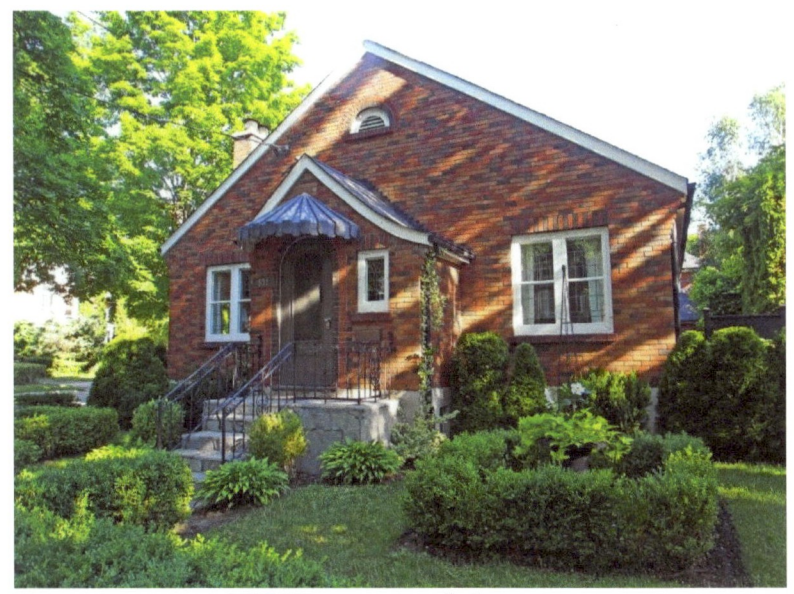

532 Homewood Avenue

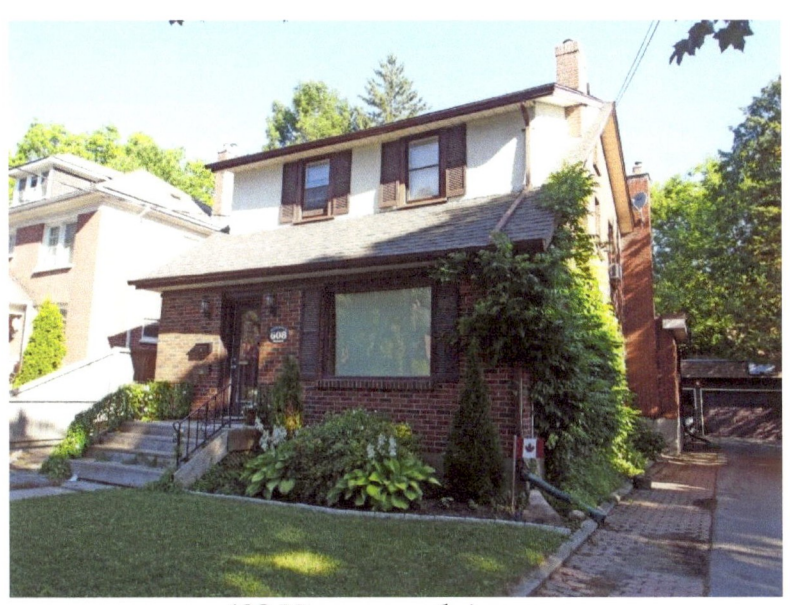

608 Homewood Avenue

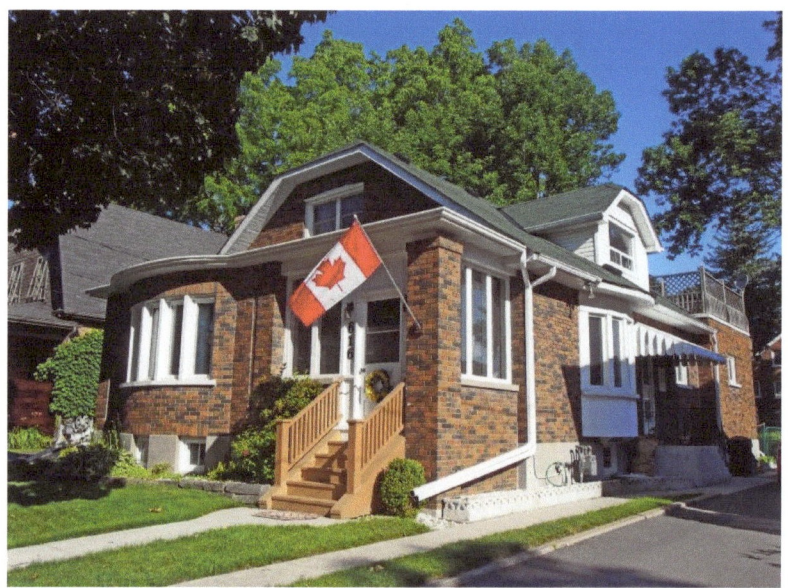

616 Homewood Avenue

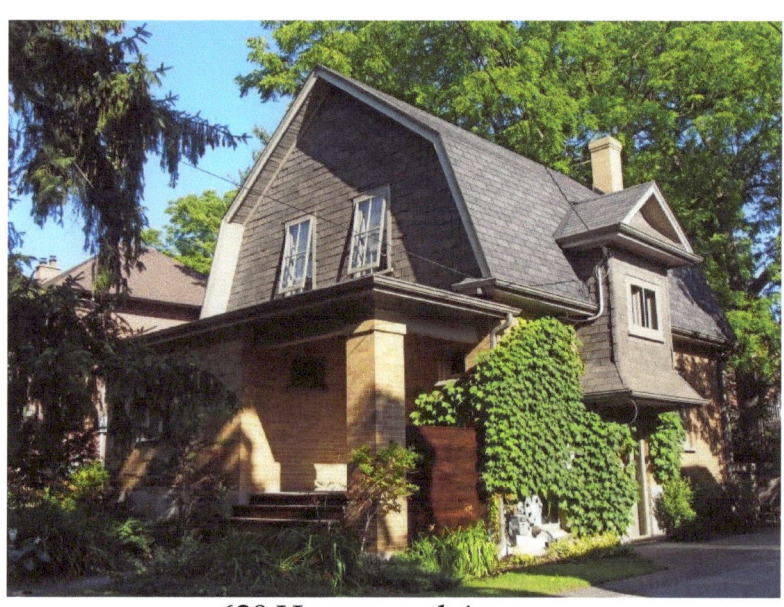

620 Homewood Avenue

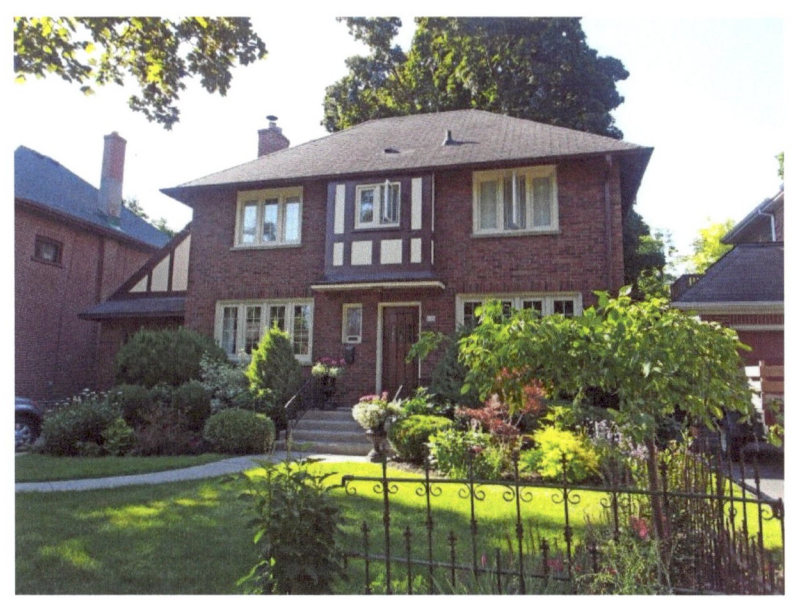

615 Homewood Avenue

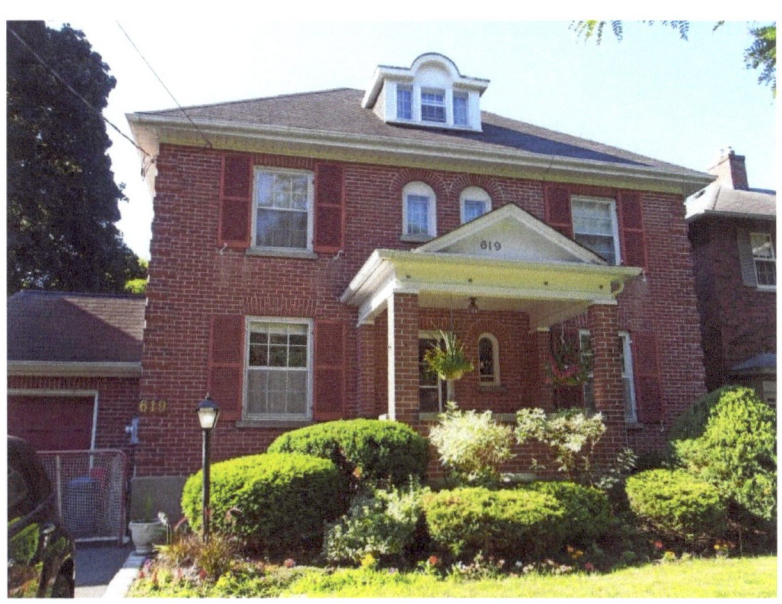

619 Homewood Avenue – Italianate, dormer, hipped roof, pediment, corner quoins

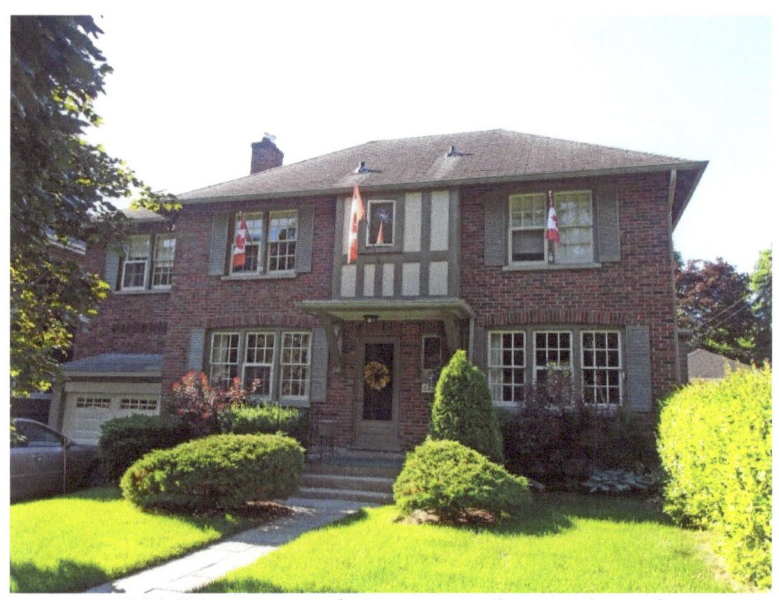

623 Homewood Avenue – hipped roof

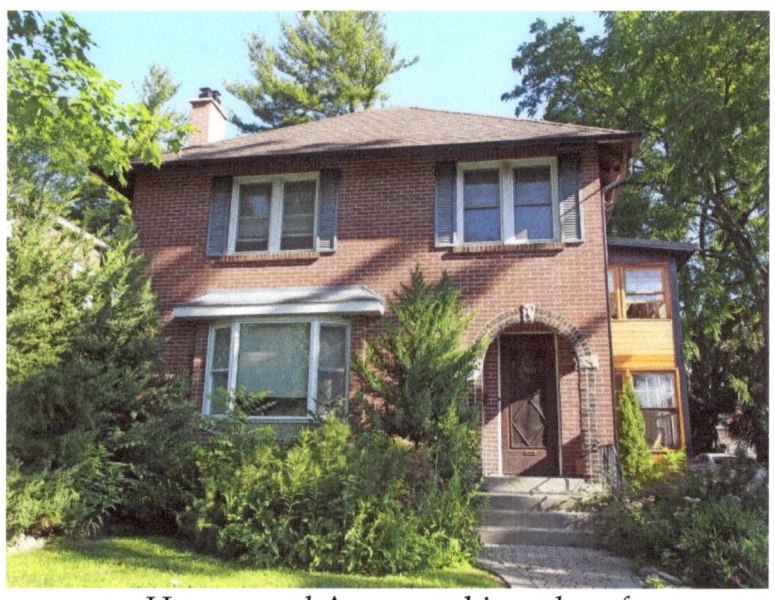

Homewood Avenue – hipped roof

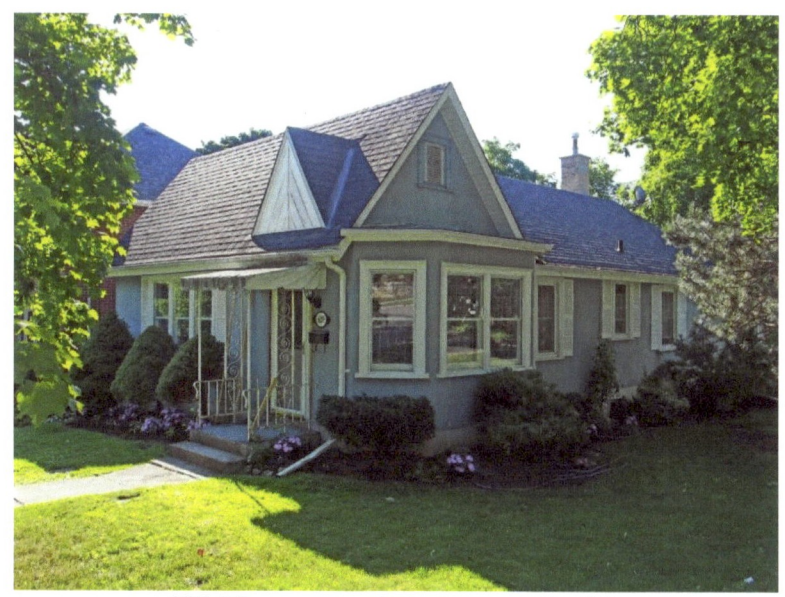

629 Homewood Avenue - Gothic

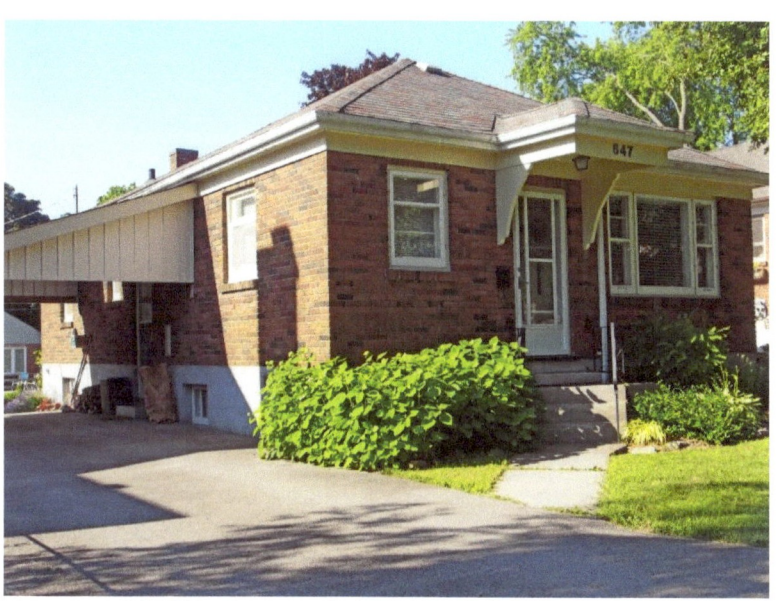

647 Homewood Avenue – hipped roof

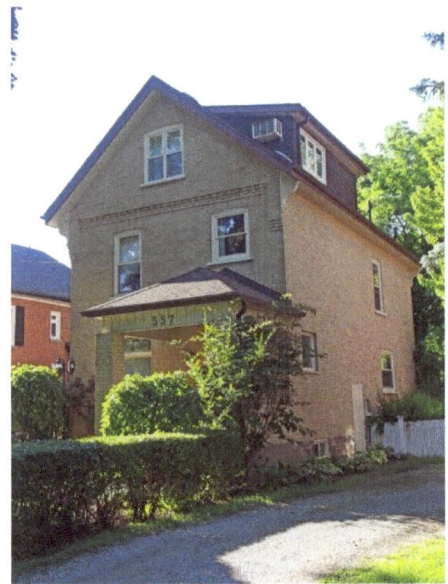

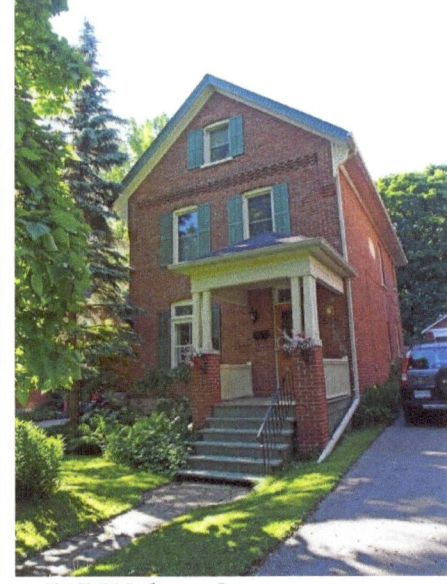

537 Walton Street   545 Walton Street
                Gothic

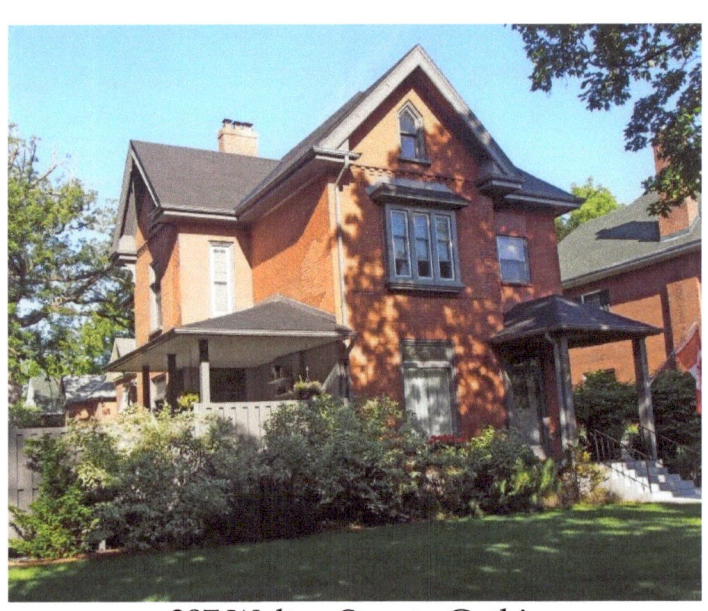

387 Walton Street - Gothic

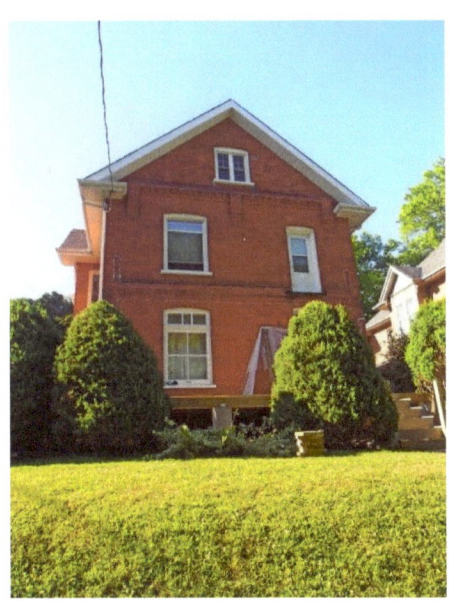

Walton Street – cornice return on Gothic gable

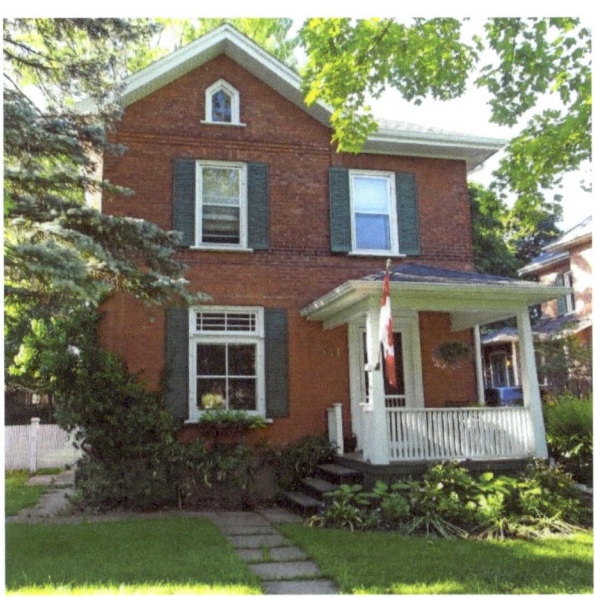

541 Walton Street - Gothic

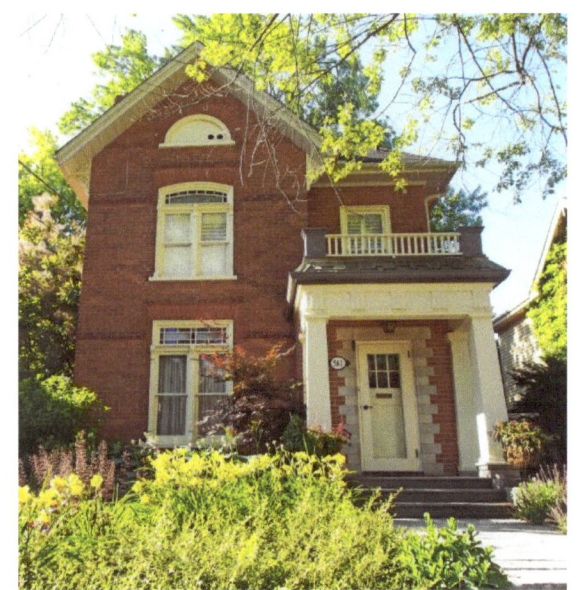

561 Walton Street – Gothic, 2nd floor balcony

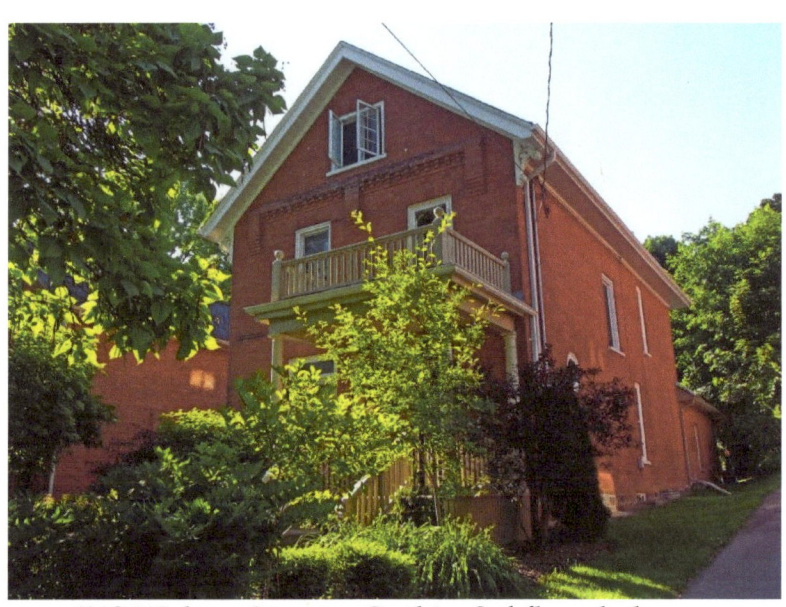

549 Walton Street – Gothic, 2nd floor balcony

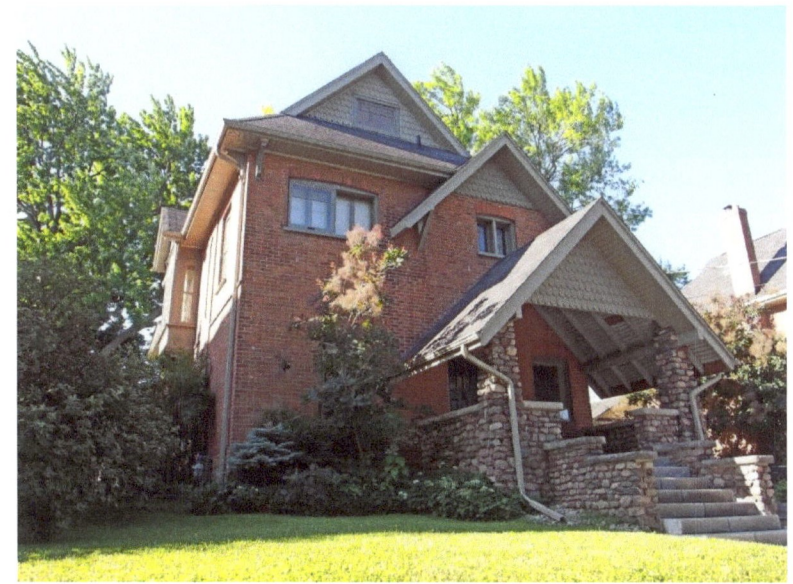

557 Walton Street

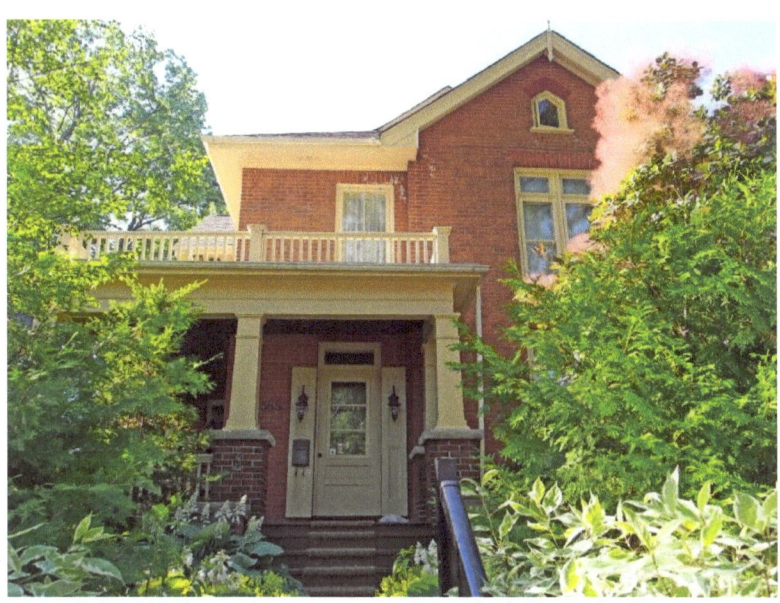

565 Walton Street – Gothic, 2nd floor balcony

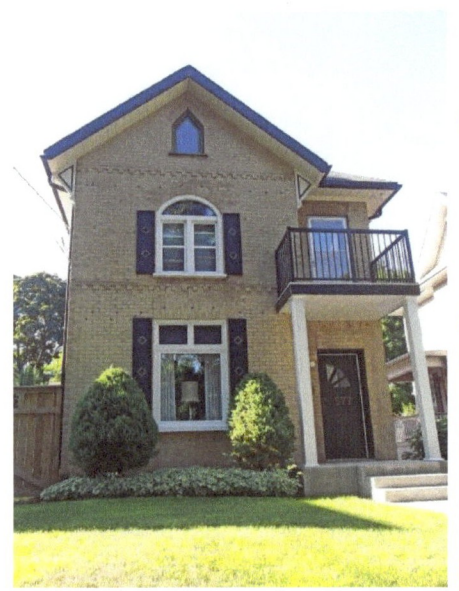

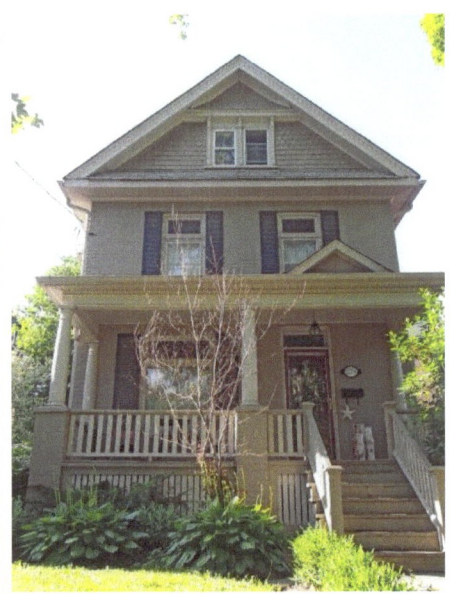

577 Walton Street
Gothic, 2nd floor balcony

579 Walton Street
Edwardian, pediment

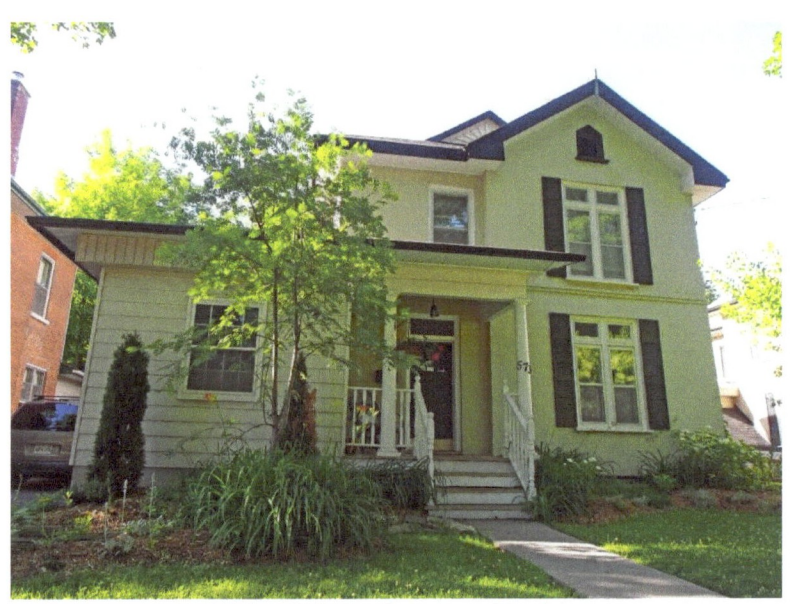

573 Walton Street - Gothic

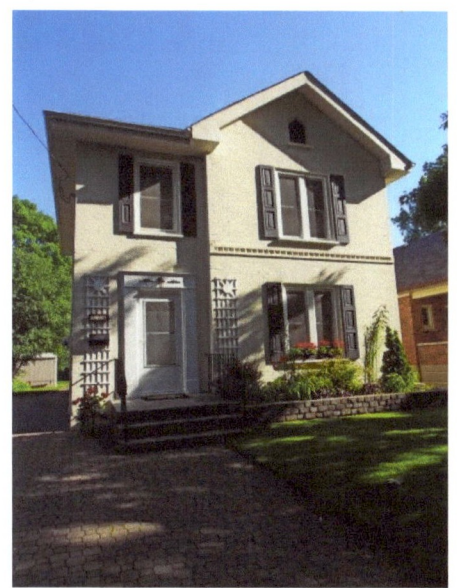

576 Walton Street

597 Walton Street
Gothic

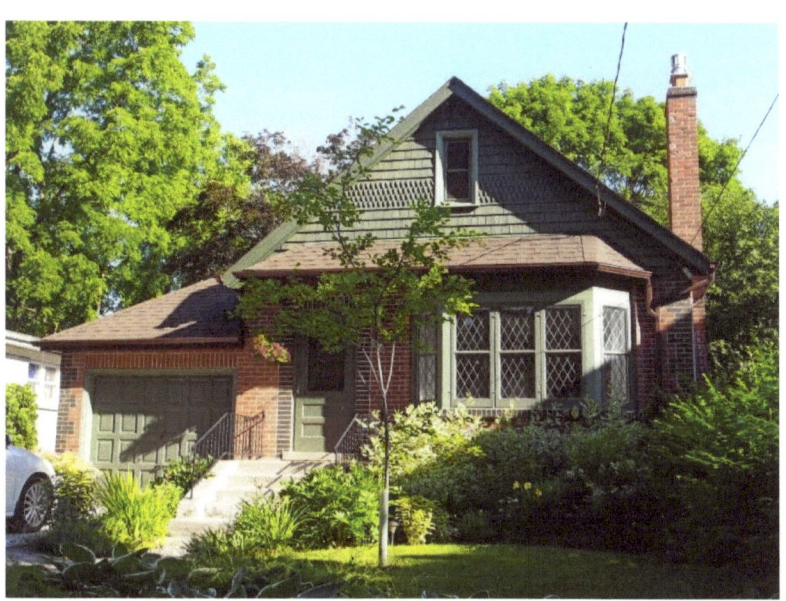

580 Walton Street - Gothic

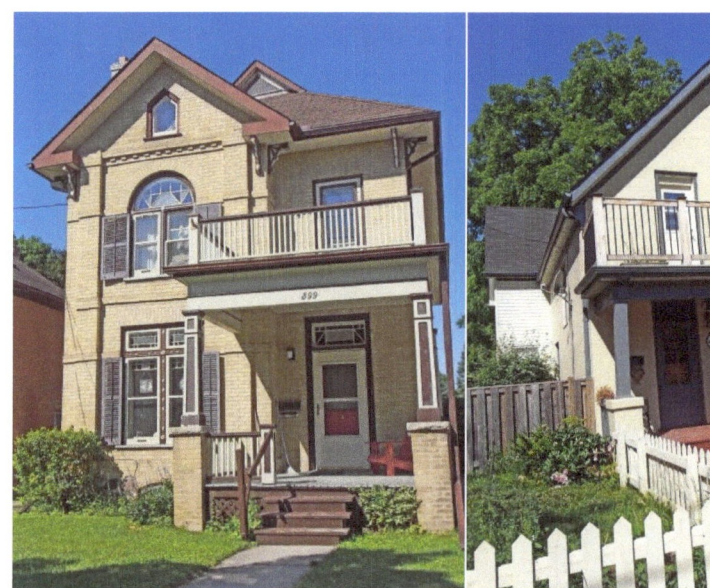

399 Walton Street
Cornice return on gable
2nd floor balcony

409 Walton Street
Gothic, 2nd floor balcony

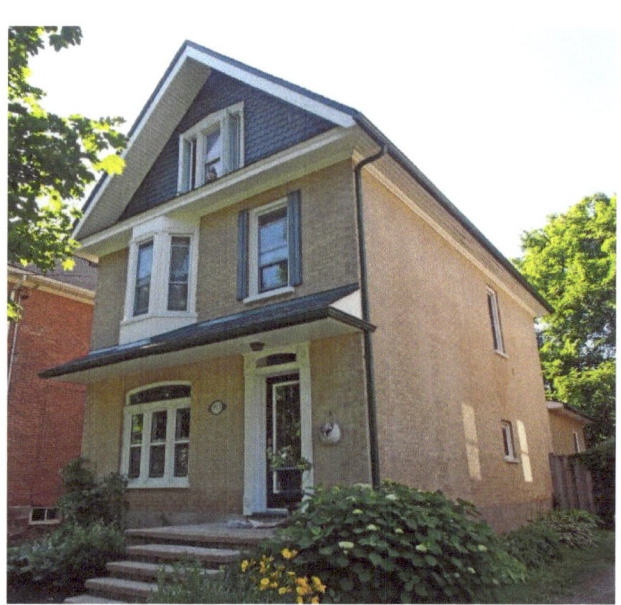

593 Walton Street - Edwardian

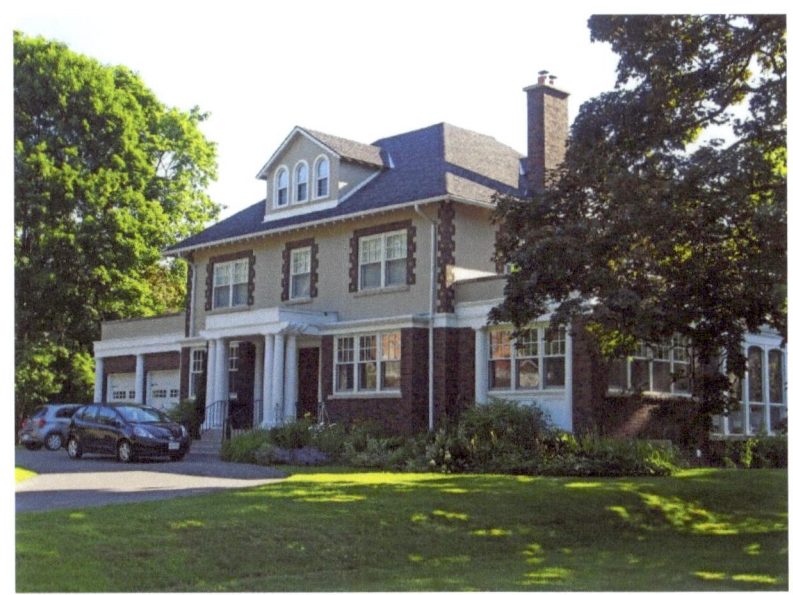

Monaghan Road – corner quoins, dormer, hipped roof

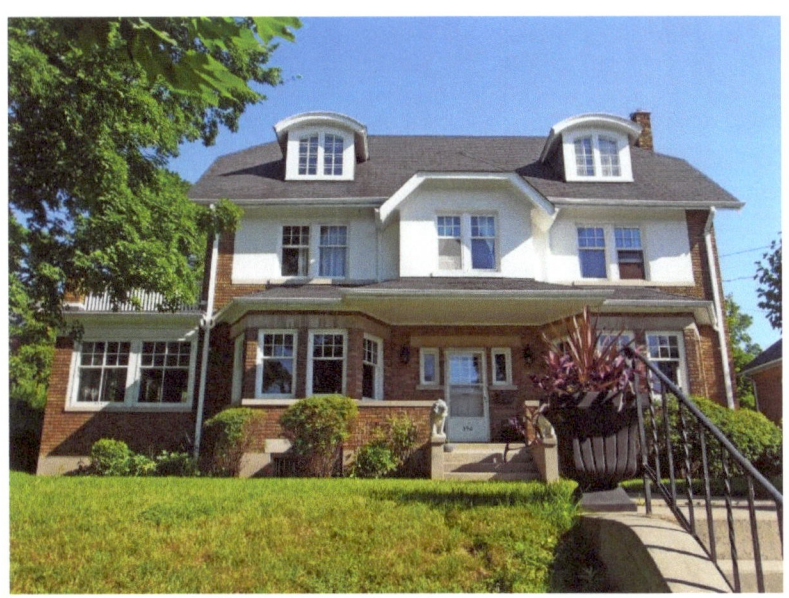

590 Weller Street - dormers

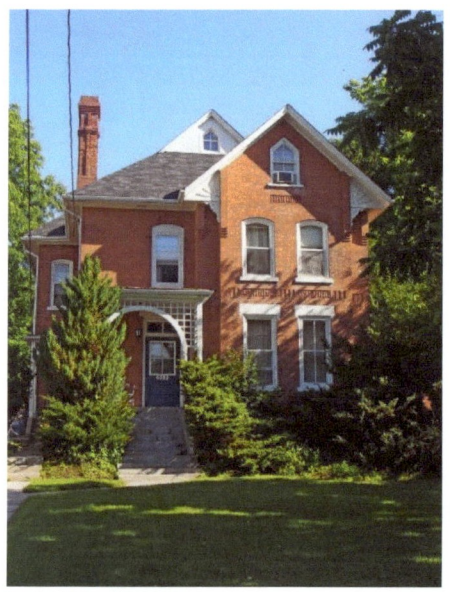

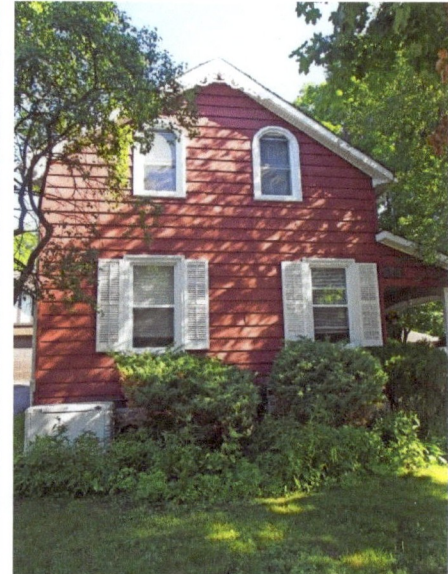

580 Weller Street   Weller Street

Gothic

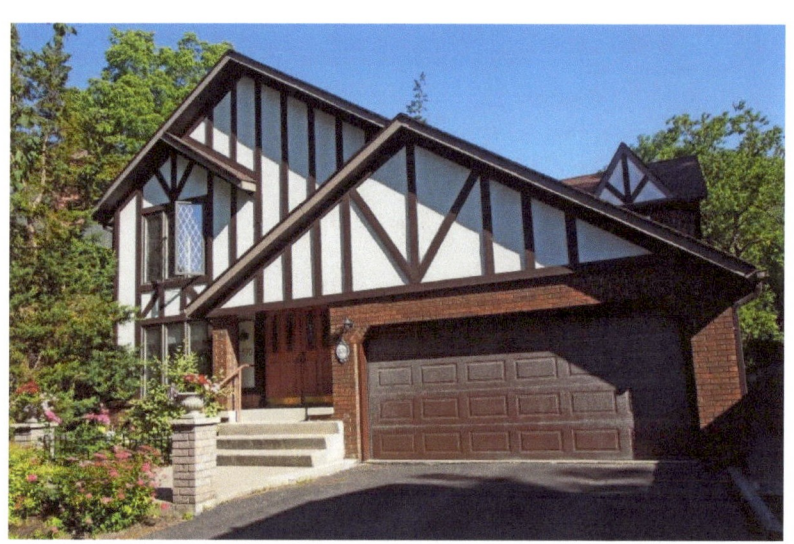

570 Weller Street - Tudor

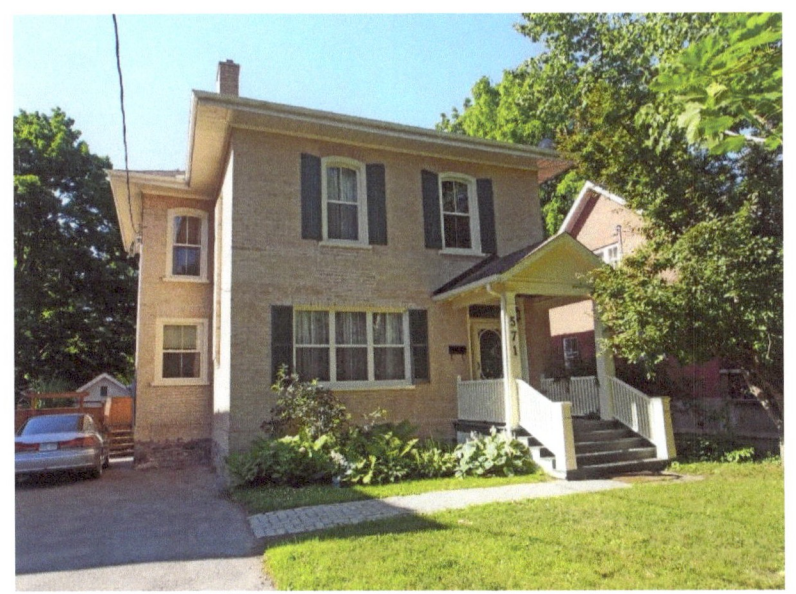

571 Weller Street – Italianate, pediment

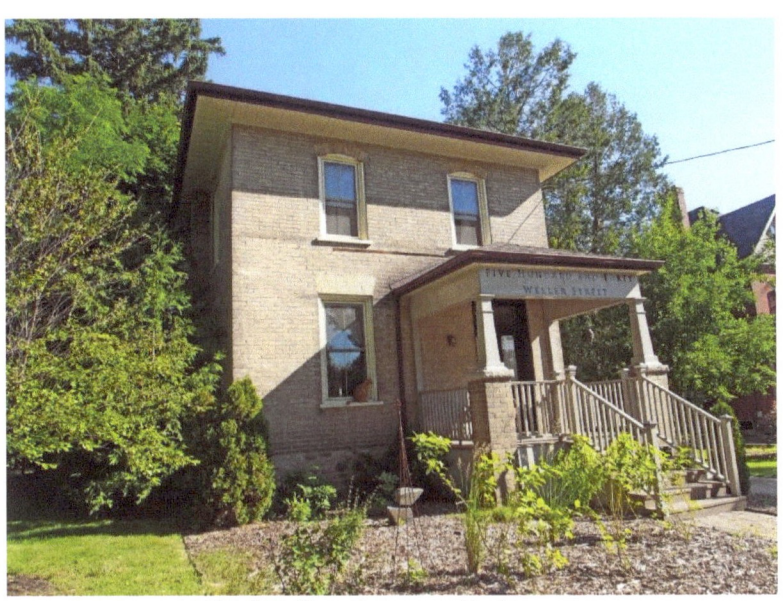

540 Weller Street - Italianate

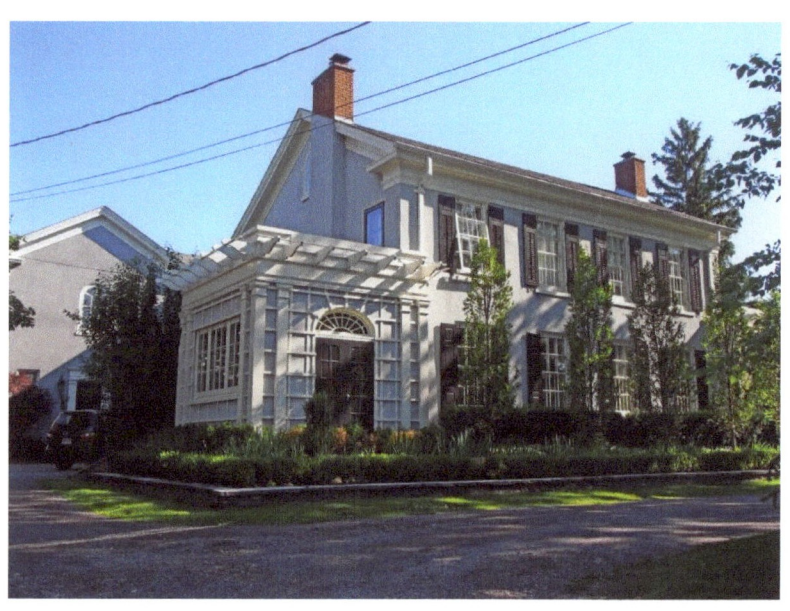

548 Weller Street – Georgian

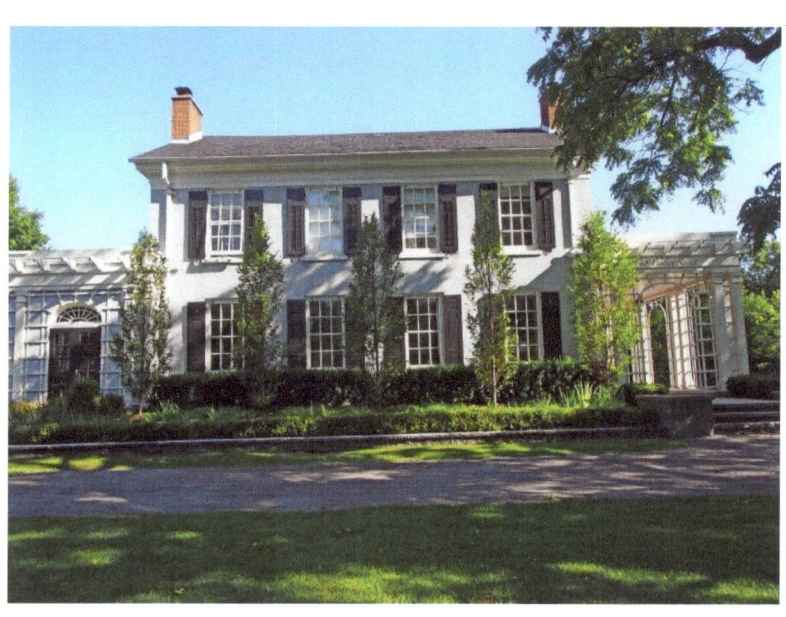

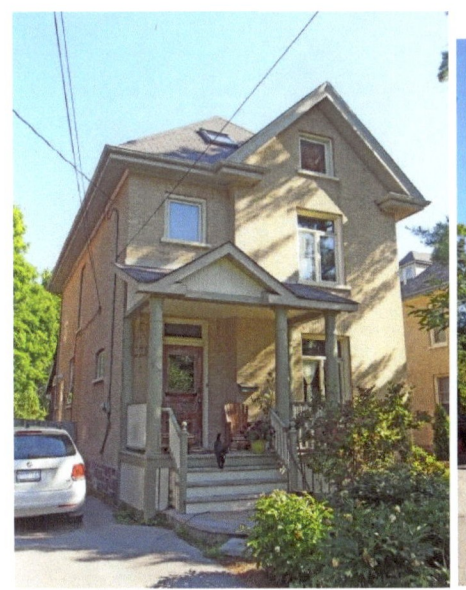

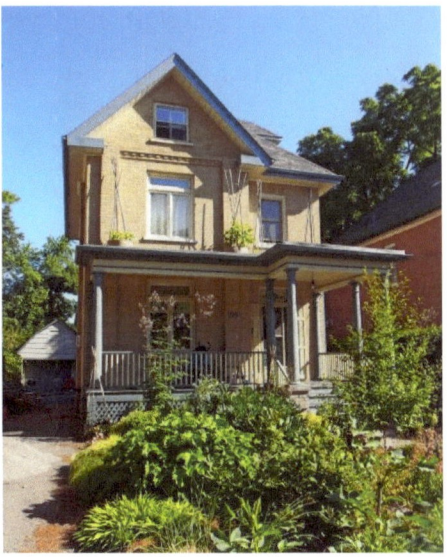

532 Weller Street
Cornice return, pediment

528 Weller Street

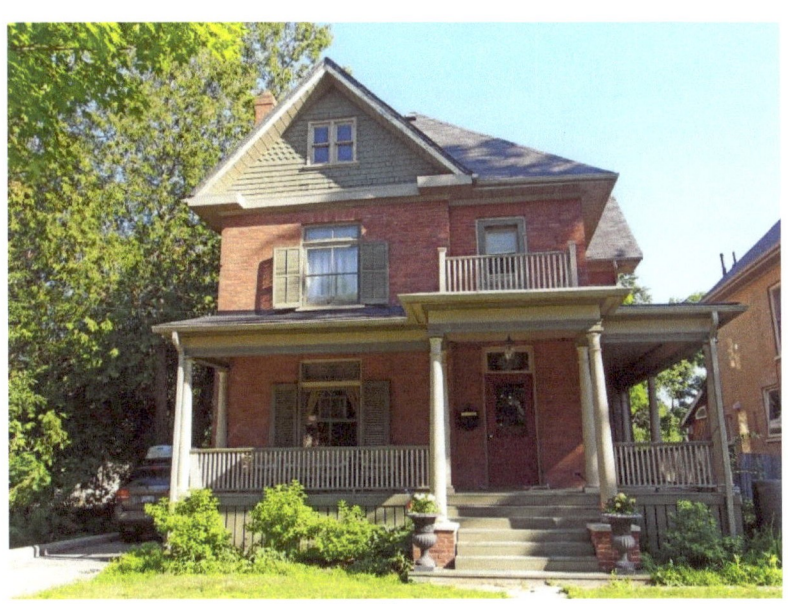

534 Weller Street

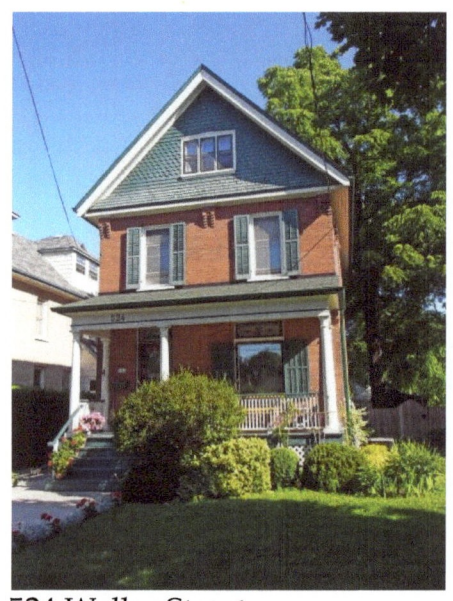

524 Weller Street
Edwardian

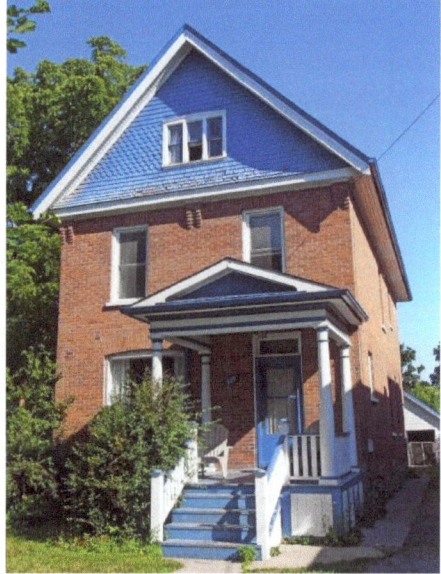

520 Weller Street - pediment

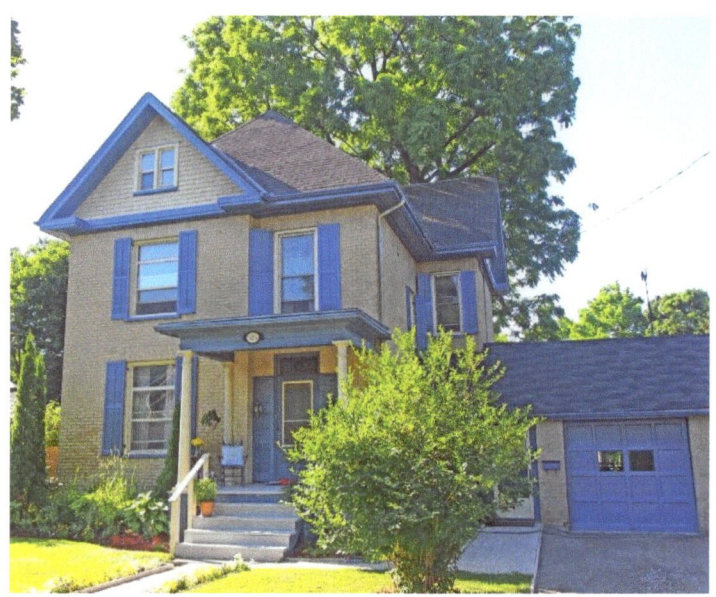

525 Weller Street – cornice return on Gable

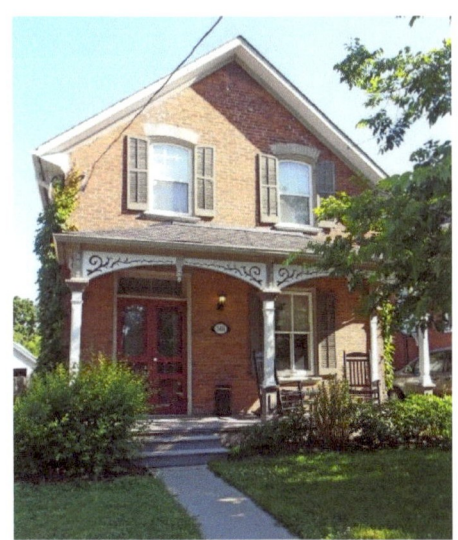

518 Weller Street - Gothic

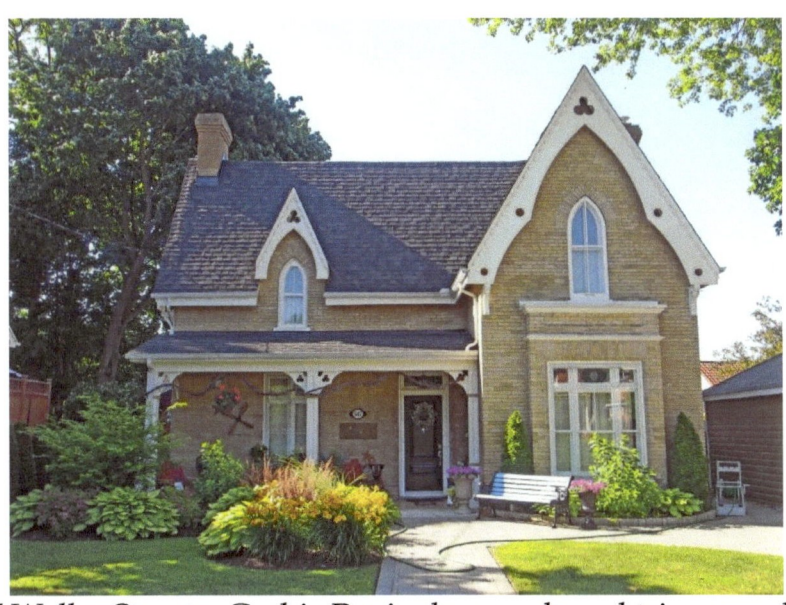

507 Weller Street – Gothic Revival, verge board trim on gables

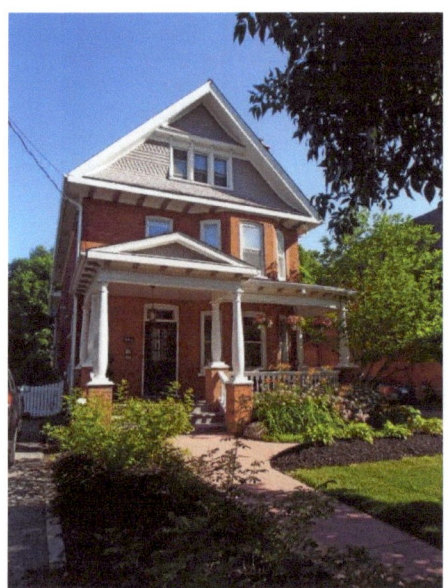 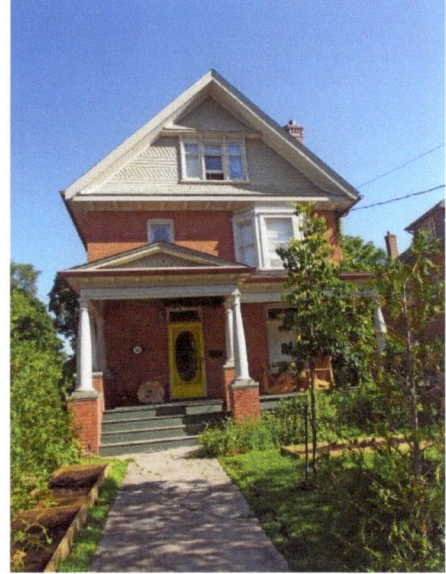

514 Weller Street   511 Weller Street

Edwardian - pediment

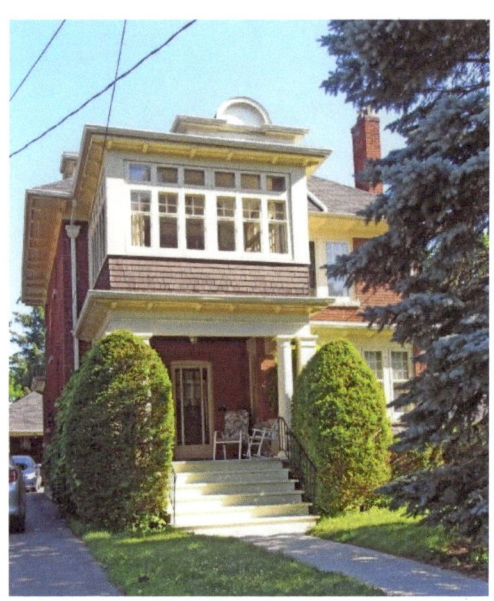

Weller Street

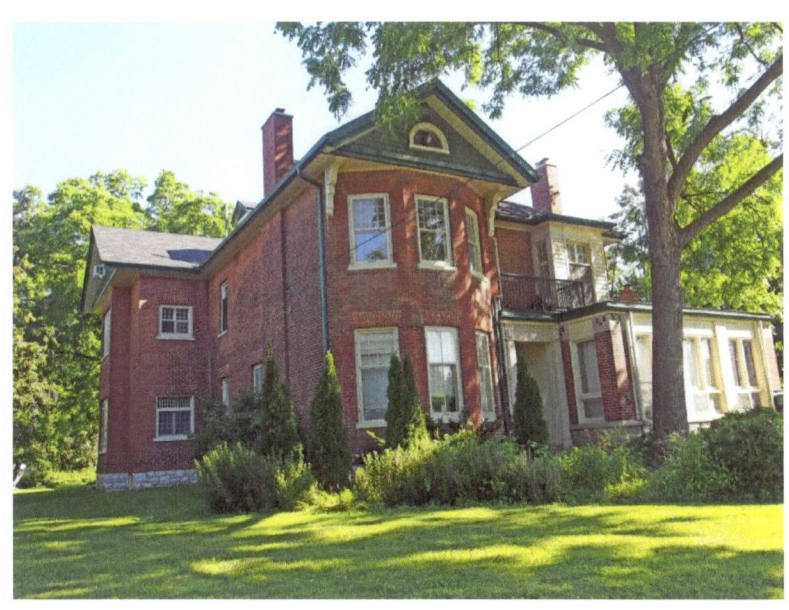

480 Weller Street – cornice brackets, 2½ storey tower-like bay

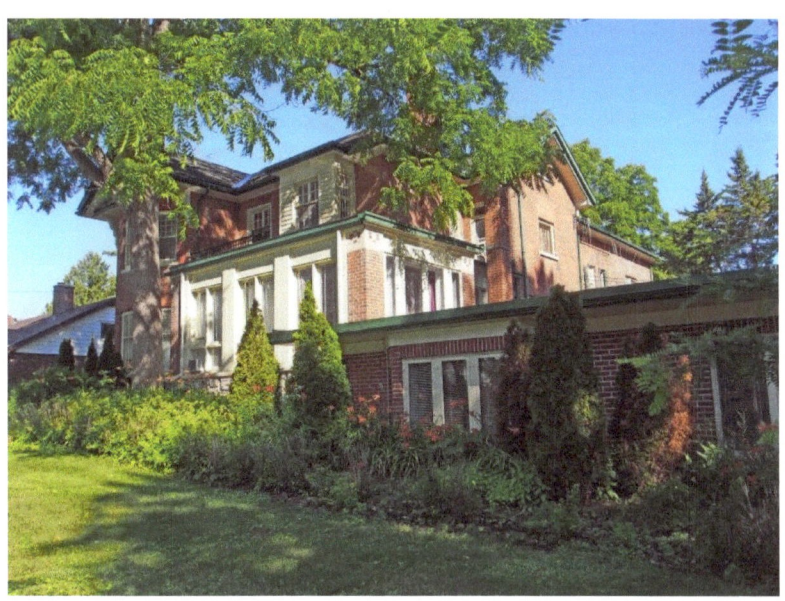

Architectural Terms

Architrave: The lowest division of the entablature (the entire horizontal mass above the columns) in classical architecture. The main lintel or beam spanning from column to column. Example: St. Peter –in-Chains Cathedral	
Belvedere: (from the Italian "beautiful view") an architectural feature on a roof, in a garden or on a terrace that gives a beautiful view. Example: 499 Homewood Avenue	
Brackets: a decorative or weight-bearing structural element which forms a right angle with one side against a wall and the other under a projecting surface such as an eave or roof. Example: 480 Weller Street	
Buttress: a masonry structure built against or projecting from a wall which serves to support or reinforce the wall. In Canadian architecture, they are sometimes used for decoration. Example: St. Andrew's United Church	
Capital: The uppermost finish or decoration on a column. An Ionic column has a small base, a thin elegant shaft, and a capital composed of volutes which are carved whirls or twists that take the form of a scroll. Example: 396 Downie Street	

Cornice Return: decorative element on the end of a gable. Example: 525 Weller Street	
Dentil Moulding: an even series of rectangles used as ornamental decoration in cornices. Example: St. Andrew's United Church	
Dormer: (French for "sleep") a gable end window that pierces through the plane of a sloping roof surface to create usable space in the top floor or attic of a building by adding headroom. Example: 619 Homewood Avenue	
Gable: the triangular portion of a wall between the edges of a sloping roof. Example: 537 Walton Street	
Hipped Roof: a roof where all sides slope downwards to the walls with no gables. Example: 619 Homewood Avenue	
Lancet Window: a tall, narrow window with a pointed arch at its top. Example: : St. Andrew's United Church	

Mansard Roof: This style was popularized by Francois Mansart (1598-1666), an accomplished architect of the French Baroque period and especially fashionable during the Second French Empire (1852-1870). This roof is almost flat on the top section, with two slopes on each of its sides with the lower slope at a steeper angle than the upper and having dormer windows. Example: 359 Downie Street	
Pediment: a triangular section above the horizontal structure (entablature), typically supported by columns. The inside of the triangle is called the tympanum. Example: 520 Weller Street	
Quoin: masonry blocks at the corner of a wall, often a decorative feature, usually larger or of a different colour than the rest of the wall.

Example: Monaghan Road | |
| **Rose Window:** a circular window with ornamental tracery radiating from the centre.

Example: St. Peter –in-Chains Cathedral | |
| **Window Hood:** A **hood** is the piece found above window openings, usually of an ornate design, and covers the top third of the opening. Hoods are commonly placed above arched or curved openings on both windows and doors. Example: 503 Homewood Avenue | |

Building Styles

Edwardian, 1900-1930 – This style bridges the ornate and elaborate styles of the Victorian era and the simplified styles of the 20th century. Balanced facades, simple roof lines, dormer windows, large front porches, and smooth brick surfaces are its characteristics. Example: 377 Downie Street	
Georgian, before 1860 – This style began with the British King Georges in the 18th century. These buildings have balanced facades around a central door, medium-pitched gable roofs, and small paned windows. Example: 548 Weller Street	
Gothic Revival, 1830-1890 – These decorative buildings have sharply-pitched gables with highly detailed verge boards, pointed-arch window openings, and dichromatic brickwork. It is a common style in Ontario. Example: 507 Weller Street	
Italianate, 1850-1900 – It has wide-bracketed eaves, belvederes, wrap-around verandahs. Example: 491 Homewood Avenue	

Second Empire, 1860-1880 – The mansard roof is the most noteworthy feature of this style and is evidence of the French origins. Projecting central towers and one or two-storey bays can also be present. Example: 359 Downie Street	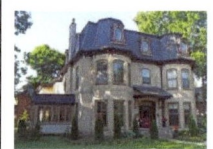
Tudor Revival – exposed timbers with stucco infill, multi-paned windows. Example: 570 Weller Street	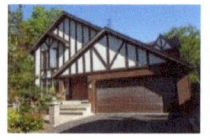

www.ingramcontent.com/pod-product-compliance
Lightning Source LLC
Chambersburg PA
CBHW040842180526
45159CB00001B/288